THE SACRAMENTS

THE
SACRAMENTS

by

CECILY HASTINGS

SHEED AND WARD
NEW YORK

Library of Congress Catalog Card Number 61-11793

NIHIL OBSTAT
    HUBERTUS RICHARDS, S.T.L., L.S.S.
        CENSOR DEPUTATUS

IMPRIMATUR
    E. MORROGH BERNARD, VIC. GEN.

WESTMONASTERII, DIE 17A MARTII, 1961

The *Nihil Obstat* and *Imprimatur* are a declaration that a book
or pamphlet is considered to be free from doctrinal or moral error.
It is not implied that those who have granted the *Nihil Obstat*
and *Imprimatur* agree with the contents, opinions or statements
expressed.

MANUFACTURED IN THE UNITED STATES OF AMERICA

CONTENTS

PART I

1. BODY AND SOUL

"I think nobly of the soul", says Shakespeare's Malvolio. And whether we dislike him on the whole for priggishness and conceit or regard him as an admirable character, much wronged, or do not happen to be acquainted with *Twelfth Night*, most of us will probably agree with him here. We think nobly of the soul; we reject materialist notions of human nature; we glory in our spirituality, our immortal destiny, our affinity with the angels, the power of mind over matter, the achievements of the mystics. If faced with someone proposing that we should talk about our souls we might, and probably would, avoid the invitation and, thereafter, the person who made it; but we should certainly assume that it was an invitation to discuss spiritual matters, the mystery of our personalities, our relationship with God, our eternal salvation. The word "soul" suggests to us something otherworldly, or at the very least "spiritual" in some sense connected with man's highest aspirations, somehow rising above the workaday material world. A Catholic finding himself involved in a discussion about the soul with people of no religious belief would probably see his task exclusively as the defence of a spiritual against a material view of man. That the soul is a spirit is a commonplace to most religious believers. It could, then, come as a shock to find that on one of the few occasions when the Church has spoken with full dogmatic authority on the subject (Council of Vienne, 1311), her concern was to insist that the soul is essentially the form of the body.

The soul is the form of the body: put thus, the statement applies to any material living thing, whether plant or animal, not only to a human being. The word "soul", *anima*, is used for that which makes some particular collection of different kinds of matter to be a living, organic unity, whether plant or animal: it is its aliveness, or, we might say, life-principle (so long as this does not lead us to think of it as a mysterious something buried within the material being). Better than that would be to start from the more ordinary English word "shape", and see how far it will take us if we, for our part, will take the idea of shape far enough. Taking it far enough means not being content with the loose approximation of calling a naturalistic statue the same shape as the man it portrays. The man has an inside as well as an outside, which is just as much his shape. Furthermore, if we had a fine enough power of vision we should see that in the shape of his body is involved the shape, both inner and outer, of every cell in it, and all their functioning, ever-changing arrangement in relation to each other. All of this is only precisely and exactly this shape so long as it is alive: a corpse is not, on a minute scale (nor, quite soon, on a larger scale either), just the same shape as the living body. It would not be possible for a mass of matter to be, in this detailed sense, precisely the same shape as a living human body except by being a living human body. Hence, to speak of "what makes it that shape" is the same as to speak of "what makes it a living human body": and in being a living human body is involved, besides mere shape, all the activities (intellectual as well as physical) which this kind of being, a human being, actually carries out. If we make a list of all the kinds of matter—carbon, hydrogen, nitrogen, calcium, etc., etc.—which there are in a human body, we then have a list of stuff which is *potentially* a human body. But here in each one of us we have that potential stuff actually *being* a body. It is this actuality of the body, *actus corporis*, which we are talking about when we speak of the form of the body, the soul.

The human soul is the form of its body; but this does not by any means imply that the human soul is not spiritual. The oddity of being human is precisely this, that in us the form by which each of us is an organically functioning material unity is also capable of activities beyond the scope of the matter which it shapes. Our soul, the form of our body, acting on every part of our material body to make it be a living body and not just so much matter, is a spirit capable of still existing (though in a diminished and unsatisfactory sense) after the decay of the body in death, and so of existing without occupying space at all. (Indeed, strictly speaking, it never occupies space: it is not distributed over the space which the body occupies but acts, whole and entire, in every part of the body.) Here and now, and hereafter, the spirit which is our soul is capable of the spirit-activities of knowing and loving, the workings of intellect and will. This is the basic truth expressed in the revelation that we are made in the image of God, for the power of a created spirit to know and to love is a reflection, though infinitely remote, of the all-knowing and all-loving Creator.

There is nothing in simply being a spirit, a

non-spatial, knowing-and-loving being, that requires it to unite with matter so as to animate
and shape it into a living body. Angels (including devils) are simply spirits, intellect and
will functioning in the fashion appropriate
to their nature, without forming any compound
with matter. Nor is there anything in simply
being an organism—matter shaped so as to be
a living body—which demands that the form
of it, its soul, shall be a spirit. On the contrary,
there is a gulf of difference between material
and spiritual being which makes their union
in one compound, when one begins to think
about it, strangely improbable. Yet man is that
compound; and it is important not to lose sight
of the unity which that compound is.

God, sheer, infinite Spirit, acts upon matter
everywhere: upon all the matter that there is,
giving it its very being; but there is no compound here. All that God creates, keeping it
in being by his powerful presence, simply is
not God. Angels, sheer spirits created by God,
can act upon matter in a variety of ways, but
they do not form a union with it. It is possible
to imagine (I believe there are legends of this
sort) an angelic spirit being compelled by God
to restrict its activity for long ages to one small
part of the material universe: say, a particular
stone. (I do not mean that such a thing has

ever happened, or that I can conceive of any reason for it to happen which would accord with God's wisdom and goodness: the example is purely for the sake of contrast.) In such a situation one could speak of the angel as acting on that stone by its presence and power, or as imprisoned in that stone: it would not *be* that stone, there would not be one single stone-angel being. All too often, Christians slide towards a notion of human nature of which this angel-stone image is a caricature. There is a tendency to speak as though the soul were a sheerly spiritual being imprisoned within the matter of the body, aspiring to rise above it and destined to be finally released from it. But the body is not the soul's prison; it is not even the soul's tool or servant, except quite metaphorically. The soul is the body's form: a human being is body shaped by spirit, and it is as truly of the soul's essence to be the body's form as to be a knowing and loving spirit. To be human is to be equally essentially matter and spirit, and we affirm this whenever we declare in the Creed that we believe in the resurrection of the body.

As this unity of the two kinds of being (matter and spirit) is in man's very nature, it runs through all his activities and experiences. Man is a spirit; he knows and loves. But it is not humanly possible to know anything or communicate any knowledge, to love or to express any love, without bodily processes being involved. Whatever extra-sensory perception may or may not be, it is not unaccompanied by material events in the brain; the most abstract thought is abstracted from sense-information; even supreme mystical experiences express themselves in the body. On the other side, the most obviously animal activities, such as breathing, moving about, eating, excretion, sexual intercourse, while not ceasing to be animal when done by a human being, are not simply the same in kind as the corresponding behaviour in any other animal, because they are done and experienced by a knowing and self-knowing, freely choosing, spiritual being, however inattentive and half-hearted or frenzied and self-forgetful he may happen at the moment to be. A man in an alcoholic stupor is not sleeping the sleep of a beast.

All human activities and experiences are both material and spiritual, for man is a matter-spirit compound unity, not a matter-spirit linked duality. If he were the latter, we should expect to find him engaged in some spiritual activities and some, distinct, material ones, and with the experiences that he enjoys similarly divided. We could hardly fail to expect, in that case, that his relationship with God, who is sheer, infinite Spirit, would belong simply in the spiritual category. But man is not this linked duality: he is matter-spirit in a compound unity; all his activities and experiences are consequently both material and spiritual, nor does this stop short of his relationship with his Creator.

Indeed, it is hard to visualize a meaning— a vocation, so to say—for such a being as man apart from this truth. As already stated, there is nothing in the nature of matter which requires it to be animated by spirit, nor anything in the nature of spirit which demands that it should animate matter. But just because matter is mere matter, and does not have the power, which is spirit's power, to know and love, the material universe cannot, of its own nature, praise and worship the God who made it. The skies declare the glory of God and the firmament proclaims the work of his hands, but they do not know that they do; it is the psalmist who knows, and lends consciousness to the worship of the stars. Man can be a mediator between God and material creation because, being spirit, he is made in the image of God and, being matter, he belongs to the material world. Nor is it enough to say this, for it is not enough to understand man's being made in the image of God simply as his possession of the power to know and to love which belongs to his own human nature. Man is meant by God to have those natural human powers, spiritual at their own level, raised to a level which could not be natural even to the highest of all created spirits. Man is made not only to enjoy natural human life at its best but to be given a share in divine life: to have union of perfect friendship with his Creator by godlike knowledge and love. Even in the preparatory, "trial-period" forms in which we have it in this life, and in which it was first given to the first members of the human race, this gift of supernatural life is already a sharing in divine life, a true friendship with God. So that man, graced with this divine gift over and above his natural possession of both spiritual and material being, was and is not only a mediator between the two created spheres of spirit and matter, but between the Creator himself and his material creation.

We catch glimpses of this in the picture of man in Paradise in the early chapters of Genesis. Man is commanded to subdue the earth, to be its lord and master: he is mediating God's lordship to the world of matter. Adam names the animals, and the name he gave each one is its name forever, says the book: a way of saying that man's mind penetrated the nature of material beings, knowing them for what they truly and permanently are. Thus the spiritual act of knowledge is mediated to matter, a truly material being coming to know other material beings as they cannot know themselves. Man is put into his Paradise garden to dress and tend it: matter is to be improved, raised to higher levels by the action upon it of spirit, and of spirit actually embodied in matter, so that the material world will be thus given fresh meaning and direction, not by some alien being but by one who is both truly a part of it and spiritual as well. And all this is in the setting of man's friendship with God, in which all that man does is part of his relationship with God, so that he is mediating to the material world his own union with the Creator.

We can say, then, that in man's unfallen state his relationship, in his very being, with matter was part of his vocation from God: part of his worship. But the humanity of which we have direct knowledge is fallen humanity, and in it we can see, in all directions, the consequences of man's compound spirit-matter nature working out through all the dislocations and wounds of sin. The radical truth about fallen humanity is that it is separated from, at odds with, God, by the attempt to be its own god. By being at odds with the Creator, it is at odds with itself—each man within himself, and all with their fellows—and with the rest of creation. There is war within man. He is spirit-shaped matter, matter-embodied spirit, and his healthy wholeness requires that this compound unity be without conflict, the matter of body always totally shaped, in all its details of movement, according to the true destiny which is recognized and accepted by the spirit, its form. But when that true destiny has been rejected, the shaping of matter by spirit goes all awry. Needs arising at the material level become cravings beyond control, too much feared to be faced. Man imprisons an abyss of unacknowledged darkness within himself, and relieves the pressure by fighting it out in hatred with his fellows, with surrounding nature, with God himself.

What healing is there? Ultimately, healing can come only from God: man has so damaged his created nature that he needs to be re-created. Nevertheless, man reaches out for healing, and the gestures with which he reaches out are still the combination of spirit and matter with which he would have worshipped God in his unfallen state. But now, instead of drawing the material world into a harmony with his own union with God, he seeks in the material world for the means to reunite himself with God and his fellow men and to reconcile himself with himself. There is nothing in the material world which can in fact do this, of course; but it can provide signs which seem to represent the longed-for reunion and bring it within reach.

So there are sacred trees which, from roots to summit, unite the lowest depth with heavenly heights; ritual dances which integrate the dancers into the movements of the heavens; washings meant to reach through flesh and bone to the very spirit; gifts and pacts and transfusions of blood to unite men with men; gifts and dedications and effusions of blood to unite men with God; communal meals in which men are one with each other through the one food they eat; sacrificial meals in which God himself enters into the same unity; images and amulets to hold divine life and power near at hand; and a whole vast multiplicity of signs embracing practically every human activity and material object.

Man, the embodied spirit, would be unable, at any rate in the fallen state in which we know ourselves, to turn his mind towards God without the mediation of some bodily image presenting the divine to him. It is a mistake to think of men as deifying the material sky: but the sky was and even remains an image mediating the eternal father to them. And, on the other hand, man would be unable to express his worship of God without resorting to material gestures and rituals, the offering of material things. Even worship which is restricted to interior thought, without outward expression, cannot exist in man without involving the matter of the brain; and the thoughts of which it is composed will inevitably be clothed in images borrowed from the material world. A man who restricts his worship to such activity has not succeeded in making it purely spiritual: he has only succeeded in excluding from it a large part of the kind of activity natural to him as a human being.

There are elements in this necessity which belong to man's fallen state, his loss of that intimacy with God in which his spiritual soul would have been enlightened. But it is not only a matter of the Fall. It is grounded in man's very nature as God means him to be, spirit and matter in one so that his every action is both spiritual and material. We may sum up by saying that even without the Fall man would have expressed his relationship with God through matter, thus mediating God to the material world and offering that world to God; but, once fallen, he can only seek God in material images and, while still using bodily things in worship, must also seek in them and their ritual use symbols which will give him an image of reconciliation with himself, his fellows, the world about him and his God.

2. EXTERNALS IN RELIGION

Such is the general foundation for a "sacramental" religion. Every action and experience of man is both bodily and spiritual, including his religious actions and experiences. Every spiritual movement in him must express itself bodily (at the very least in his brain, however outwardly repressed); every bodily experience must affect him spiritually to some degree. Let us, then, neither ignore nor minimize our nature, but gladly accept reality with its full consequences. Let there be sacrament and ceremonial, processions and palm-branches, lights and incense, ritual robes and music, sculpture and architecture and painting and coloured glass, pilgrimages and shrines and medals and relics and everything with which man has ever expressed the sacred in his life. For if all these things are banished and not used to lead us towards God, they will reappear elsewhere and lead us away from him. They are part of our nature as God created it; let us reconsecrate it all to him.

But an objection should occur to us here. Suppose that it is agreed that this kind of religion is natural to man, or that at least it always has come naturally to him. But when we speak of God mediated in an image, are we not condoning precisely the idolatrous development of religion which St. Paul condemns in the Epistle to the Romans? Is not the line of development, in God's chosen people, from ceremonial religion to ethical religion? Do not the Prophets represent an advance upon the ritualism that went before them, and do they not reject sacrifice and ceremony altogether in favour of the worship given by a morally good life? "I desire not holocausts of rams and fat of fatlings ... Offer sacrifice no more in vain: incense is an abomination to me ... Learn to do well: seek judgement, relieve the oppressed, judge for the fatherless, defend the widow." (Isa. 1.11–17.) Was there not already a preparation for this spiritualizing of religion, even in the most external, ritual stage of the revelation to the Hebrews, in the absolute prohibition of image-making? And is not all this confirmed and sealed by Jesus Christ himself, who, besides condemning the external observances of the Pharisees, announced the end of the Temple worship by saying that "God is a spirit, and they that adore him, must adore him in spirit and in truth"? (John 4.24.)

The danger of idolatry is real enough. Like the temptation to every other sin, it is part of the fallen state of humanity. The temptation is to change from worshipping God as mediated to us in an image to stopping short at the image so that it usurps the place of God. It is not images as mediating God to us that St. Paul condemns. He uses them himself. "Father-hood", so far as we can understand the word, is such an image; so is "the body of Christ", and so on with all the other images abounding in Paul's letters. What he condemns is a pagan-ism which allowed its images to become stale and meaningless, instead of renewing the sense of the invisible divine reality beyond them, a paganism which "*changed* the glory of the in-corruptible God into the likeness of the image ... *changed* the truth of God into a lie; and worshipped and served the creature rather than the Creator". (Rom. 1.23–5.) But there was an original awareness there to be changed, a wor-ship to be corrupted, an awareness and a worship which were always mediated by images: only later came the change, the stop-ping short at the image which corrupted it into an idol.

The prohibition of the making of images (in the sculptural sense) was so far from being absolute that explicit exceptions were made to it—a brazen serpent, carved cherubim. It was a vitally necessary safeguard of the chosen people, surrounded by a world of worn-out, idolatrous images, since their task was to bear witness, in contrast to their surroundings, to the invisible God. But, besides being neither permanent nor without exceptions even at the time, it involved no general rejection of the mediating role of images. The whole of Hebrew literature in which God's revelation is conveyed is one mass of verbal imagery and a continuous recognition of the necessity and validity of material signs in man's relationship with God: the Ark, the Tabernacle, the Temple, the sacrifices, the special celebrations of different feasts, the music and processions and incense and vestments of the Temple worship.

But while the rejection of the bodily nature of man is simply a rejection of the truth about him and his true relationship to God, this obviously does not mean that so long as man's worship does take a material form it can automatically be regarded as satisfactorily religious. Man is not just matter; he is *spirit-shaped* matter. His activities are only fully human, and can only be truly religious, when they are material, indeed, but fully shaped, given their meaning and their inner reality by the spirit. This is why the Prophets rail against sacrifices which injustice and impiety have emptied of meaning; and it is precisely because their meaning is sacred that to empty them of meaning is such a blasphemous insult to God. Isaias, who records the scene of his vocation in the holy place, when he saw the Lord enthroned in the neglected Temple, and when the prophet's own lips were cleansed for his coming task with a burning coal from the altar of sacrifice, was certainly not rejecting the sacredness of the Temple, but calling for a renewal of it. When ritual has become a perfunctory performance, and life goes on with God and his law ignored, then the meaning of ritual has gone out of it; it is no longer a shaping of matter by spirit, and the prophet must cry that such sacrifice is useless and life itself must be remodelled according to the law before sacrifice can have meaning again. But this does not imply a rejection of "ritual religion" for "ethical religion". Both are part of human life, and either can become an idolatry. Indeed, since in "ethical religion" the image through which God is being mediated is that of good human behaviour, it makes ritual's deep and humble assertions of human needs and dependences, going far beyond the range of conscious behaviour, more urgently needed than ever. For the idolatry into which ethical religion can fall is the worst of all idolatries: the direct worship of man by himself.

Christ our Lord himself certainly cannot be pressed into the service of a rejection of material images and of the mediation of matter in religion, without ignoring almost the whole story. Indeed, the whole story, without any "almost"; the story is that of God deliberately choosing to make a human body, voice, eyes, hands, feet, the medium by which he would communicate finally and completely with man. And lest we should think that this was merely a sort of necessity (given our condition), grudgingly accepted, so to speak, and to be ignored as far as possible, he made it clear, on the contrary, that he delighted in it. He went out of his way, you might say, in several of his miracles, to bring a particularly earthy sort of material medium into the act: clay and spittle are not exactly suggestive of a spirituality which would leave bodily things out of it. He accepted the Magi's gifts, showed us the symbolism of Mary's anointing, arranged the first procession of palms. Like all the revelation that had gone before, his teaching is a tissue of verbal imagery, weaving the things of the material world into a manifestation of spiritual truth. His talk to the woman at the well in Samaria, when he said that God is a Spirit and must be worshipped in spirit and truth, was built on the theme of an age-old, healing, material-spiritual symbol: lifegiving water. In the light of what he was and all that he did and said, we know that we are not playing with words when we say that to worship God in spirit and in *truth* must mean, for us human beings, to worship him in spirit and through matter, with matter, giving matter a spiritual meaning and bringing it into our worship: for the truth about us is that we are matter as well as spirit, embodied spirits.

3. THE MEANING OF SACRAMENTS

The heat and dust of controversy have, unfortunately, risen at various times over some of the consequences of the general truth sketched over the last few pages: that a truly human religion, and hence true Christianity, must be a religion of matter as well as of spirit. But there is something, at least, which is common ground amongst Christians in general: that our Lord did make this religious use of matter a part of the Christian life in at least the two great acts of baptism and the Eucharist. Here we have, at the very least, the high point, the consecration by Christ himself, of the ritual and, in a wide sense, "sacramental" use which man has made of matter throughout the history of religion. Here we have two tremendous symbols, related to two fundamentals in our natural biological life, birth and nourishment: the symbols of water, and of food and drink. Water signifies much more than mere washing. It is a flood in which an old world, an old life, can be drowned and disappear, and a womb from which new life can come forth, as life first emerged from the seas of this planet. And food and drink, too, are much more than mere rations. A banquet is an act of the community; food and drink are unifying, they nourish not only life but the common life; companionship means eating together, taking our *panis*, bread, in common.

These two symbols at least Christ took, filled with his own meaning, and enjoined upon his followers. It would be easy to write in very general terms about them in such a way as to make the agreement among all sorts of Christians on this matter seem greater than it is. It is necessary, on the contrary, to make the real cleavage appear as clearly as possible, since agreement based on misunderstanding is no unity at all but only a profitless talking at cross-purposes.

The way to blur the difference would be to say, or imply, that the sacraments are simply the supreme example of the religious use of material things, giving them a spiritual meaning, which flows from the nature of man as a body-soul unity. Visible, material signs work upon man as a spirit by the way in which they naturally affect his body, and through that the soul which animates it. Christ, we should be saying if we took this line, was simply using this means, which is part of the very nature of man, in the most perfect way possible. The signs of baptism and the Eucharist work on man's spirit in the same way as all other visible signs work on him: they are the most effective possible signs, because they are the ones chosen for us by Christ who is God, who perfectly knows us and the workings of our nature: but the mode of their working is still simply what we should nowadays call psychological.

I have now pushed this notion of the meaning of the sacraments to the point where it is no longer blurred but clearly cut off from and opposed to the Catholic doctrine. The Catholic doctrine here, moreover. means also the doctrine which is held by the Eastern Orthodox, other Christians of the East, and even by many groups and individuals in the West who have, within a general framework of Protestantism, yet either retained or recovered the Catholic idea of the meaning of the sacraments. But the opposite, the "purely psychological" idea sketched above, can be called the Protestant idea of sacraments as being characteristic of the Reformation movement: it can be found clearly stated by Calvin, for instance. In that idea, sacraments can be called a kind of preaching. They are signs which speak to the soul through the body, and they contribute to life in Christ in just the same way that preaching does; by their psychological effect leading, as a motive power, to Christian living.

It is an idea which could well be carried to greater depths, today, than it could be in Calvin's day, now that much more is known of how symbols (such as "rebirth from water") can work in the depths of the human mind, far below consciousness, with a healing and releasing power. It might even be possible to work out a theory of sacraments, on a basis of depth psychology, by which the name of "sacrament" would belong precisely to those signs which do have the power of working deep in the unconscious (true symbols), whereas lesser signs and ceremonies, lacking such power, would not deserve the name. We should say, in that case, that all signs work psychologically, but some work at the conscious level (which we

might call pious customs, or sacramentals, etc.),
while others, as Christ well knew when he instituted them, work deep in the unconscious, and
these we call sacraments.

This is not, however, the distinction between
sacraments and other religious signs which
holds good in Catholic doctrine, as it has been
from the beginning, in East and West alike.
What we say is that all signs work psychologically, whether at a conscious or unconscious
level; but there are seven signs, given by Christ,
which work not only psychologically but also in
a way entirely special to themselves and strictly
supernatural; and these are the sacraments.
The basic natural inter-workings in man of
spirit and matter underlie the sacraments, indeed. The nature of man, with its consequences
in the relationship of spirit and matter, is of
course presupposed by God in his sacramental
plan. But the sacraments themselves are not
merely the supreme example of this relationship; they are rooted in it but go beyond it.
If they did not go beyond it, they would be,
indeed, of little use to us. For all that signs and
symbols can do by their natural power is to
show us an *image* of the union with God for
which we long. Christ came to give those long-
ings fulfilment. Hence his signs do not merely
give an image of union with God, psychologi-

cally preparing the mind for grace: they **give**, through the image, the *reality* of our union with God, grace itself.

We should introduce some technical phrases here. All the signs and ceremonies which the Church uses for inspiration and self-expression, simply because of the material-spiritual nature of man, strengthen our life in Christ only in the manner described in the phrase *ex opere operantis*, "by the action of the doer". So far as they speak to us psychologically, so far as we use them devoutly so as to stimulate our devotion, they can and do help. But there is no power in them beyond this. They can work only in the way the Reformers held that the sacraments work.

We, on the other hand, hold that the sacraments work *ex opere operato*, "by the action done". We do not benefit simply from the devotion that we contribute, plus the natural effect of a helpful external sign. We benefit from the unfailing action of God, giving grace of a certain kind and for a certain purpose wherever and whenever the act is done which he himself has made into a sacred and effective sign.

This is the point where someone may murmur "magic". But that is a name for operations which, while they are believed by their performers to be effective "by the action done", are certainly of a very different nature from the sacraments. There is not necessarily just one belief for which the word "magical" is used; I suppose that it would apply equally well, for instance, to the theory that there are forces entirely natural in their workings (conceived in much the same way as we think of, say, electricity) which can be harnessed and employed by certain actions; and to the theory that certain performances can bind powerful spirits to the magician's service. And I do not suppose that these two can necessarily be clearly marked off from each other. But whichever were held, or whatever combination of them, such a theory is totally different from our sacramental belief. We do not hold that the sacraments are naturally capable of harnessing any force for any purpose whatever, but that they are signs through which the all-powerful God freely chooses to act. Nor do we believe that they are means by which we "bind" the Holy Spirit to our will; on the contrary, by *his* will we perform them, and through them he freely acts. It may further be said that, in general, magical rites are performed to achieve some material end, often destructive or even murderous; whereas sacraments are performed that God may achieve a spiritual end in us. Magical ceremonies are believed to be effective by a natural, though secret, power for material ends. Sacraments are ceremonies believed to be effective by no power of their own but by God's intervention, for spiritual ends. The point of resemblance, such as it is, consists only in their both being ceremonies which are believed to be effective, while the way in which they are believed to be effective, and the effect itself, are quite different in kind.

Sacraments do not operate, then, by some inherent, natural, though secret power; that would be magic. Nor do they operate by natural psychological power, as part of the general interworking of matter and spirit in man, as I have said already in connection with the Reformers' ideas. Then in what sphere of causes and effects do they belong? The answer is that their working is in the supernatural order. Their effectiveness belongs to that sphere of God's action in which he, who has created all things with their own natural existence and powers, gives over and above this, to us humans, a life which is above our nature, supernatural. It is divine life; it could not be natural even to an angel; by nature, it could be lived only by God. Sharing in this life, we can know God by divine knowledge, love him with love like his own, and other beings in him. This life is given to us to live already, by faith, in this world, and to be fulfilled in the vision of God hereafter. And it is given to us in Christ.

Christ is God the Son, truly God our creator, becoming and remaining in his own person a true member of the human race, material body and spiritual soul, like ourselves. That material body, literally the body of God the Son, was the thing in which he, by dying, rising again bodily, and taking that body into glory, united the human race with God so that we could live with divine life. Furthermore, the meaning of his church is that he continues to live and work in the world bodily. The Church is his body: not indeed the physical body, born of Mary, in which he walked in Palestine, but truly his body in a vital, organic and not just institutional and organizational sense. It is not simply "God's body of men", meaning God's society, a society ruled and guaranteed by the supreme Spirit: it is *Christ's* body, the body of Christ in his human nature, Christ who belongs to our world of matter and spirit. This visible, very human thing, the Church, is united to Christ the Head so that it is truly his living body still present in this world; his flesh and his bones, as St. Paul says. (Eph. 5.30.) Its acts, of which the sacraments are the most essential, are his acts. And as his natural body has been glorified in his resurrection, so our bodies too are similarly to rise again, at the end of this world's history, to share in his glory when he comes again.

Throughout all this we have the body, which belongs to the material order, not only united with something belonging to the spiritual order, as it naturally is in human beings, but raised above this to the supernatural order. Christ's natural human body was not merely formed by spirit, as any human body is, by his natural human soul, but supernaturalized, raised to the supernatural order by its personal union with the eternal Word and the fullness of divine grace filling Christ's human soul. And it is by the sacrifice, resurrection and glorification of that body, working on down the ages through his body the Church, that we are redeemed, body and soul. We are raised, body and soul, into the supernatural order, though this work is only to be finished in us on the Last Day.

It is to this divine economy, centred on Christ's body, that the sacraments, bodily signs and actions, belong. The one great Sacrament is the Word-made-flesh; God himself in material-spiritual human nature, who was and is and is to come. It is in virtue of that one great sacrament that the seven sacraments, material-spiritual in nature, communicate God to us. Hence all the sacraments are rooted three times over in the history of redemption. All of them are, in a mysterious way, making present the Word-made-flesh in his redemptive life, death, resurrection and ascension; while they are at the same time acts of Christ in his body the Church, building us into that body in which we are here and now living the life of God by grace; and they are also looking forward to and preparing us for the second coming of Christ, in which the redemption of our bodies will be completed.

4. THE SEVEN SACRAMENTS (1)

Even if we have glimpsed the vision of that which Christ accomplished in his body being communicated to us in his body the Church through bodily signs, leading eventually to the redemption of our own bodies, it is by no means obvious why there should be seven signs. While it is fairly puzzling that the medieval Catharist heretics, who regarded all matter as simply evil, should have had any sort of sacrament at all, it is perfectly understandable that they should have regarded one as sufficient. It is equally intelligible that Protestants at the time of the Reformation should have reduced the

seven to two, not only because these two, baptism and the Eucharist, are the greatest of the
seven and the ones to which the New Testament witness is clearest, but also because there
is a simple, obvious, common sense in having
a sacrament to initiate Christian life and a
sacrament to sustain it, but nothing like so
tidy a pattern into which the seven, with their
varied particular objects, can be fitted.

We have the authoritative teaching of the
Church (witnessed to by East as well as West
and, finally, dogmatically stated at the Council
of Trent) that the sacraments are indeed seven,
and just these seven. We do not have any
authoritative teaching which would illuminate
why it should be just so: Christ made it so, but
we have no precise explanation why. Nevertheless, there is an indication of an answer that
is especially connected with the sacraments as
the remedy for sin; that is, for the wounds in
our fallen human nature.

Our nature is complex, and the Fall has
wounded it in many different ways. One reason
why the sacramental scheme is complex and
multiple is that it is working on our human
nature at all the points where it is wounded.
The fundamental wound is original sin, the
sheer lack of the life of God in which we are
created to share; and this is remedied in

baptism. But restoring our share in God's life still leaves our nature damaged: in its weakness it is liable to relapse and need mending again (penance), and needs always to be strengthened and nourished (the Eucharist). One of the weaknesses in fallen humanity is self-centredness; even with spiritual goods there is a tendency to hug them to ourselves, to turn inwards. Confirmation is the sacrament of witness, of the life of the Church turned outwards to the world around. The misuse of authority, whether governing or teaching authority, is one symptom of a wound in our nature: holy orders is healing applied to that wound. Sickness is a consequence of sin, and so again a symptom of the Fall: hence the anointing of the sick. And one of the most severely wounded aspects of man's nature is his sexual life; hence the sacrament of marriage.

We may feel we could think of other wounds, so why not other sacraments? But can we really think of needs that are not met? Man is surely as badly wounded in his economic as in his sexual life; that comes down to food and drink in the end, and we can see that the Eucharist is at work on the wound. The abuse of our powers of speech is another symptom: but we have the sacraments of teaching (orders), witness (confirmation) and self-accusation (penance) at work on it. Our relationship with our parents? There are marriage, and holy orders, which, by conferring spiritual fatherhood, sheds light on the meaning of parenthood. With our equals, companions? This brings us back to the Eucharist. Perhaps it is almost possible to see how our damaged humanity is being worked on by the seven sacraments together so that neither fewer nor more of them are needed.

We should, however, realize that the Church did not finally count her seven unique treasures for several centuries. In the West, the definite listing of the seven only took place in the Middle Ages, from about the twelfth century. Earlier, we find St. Augustine, for instance, apparently regarding the washing of the feet as a sacrament, the ceremony which we have today as part of the Mass of Maundy Thursday. In the early Middle Ages the coronation of a king was regarded by some as a sacrament. On the other hand, some of our seven were not always thought of in the same light. Marriage was not seen as a sacrament for some centuries, and then in the East earlier than in the West.

This is not to say, however, that the Church's doctrine has changed. It is not that there has been, from the beginning, a definite doctrine of sacraments, but disagreement between theologians, or between different periods, about the number of them. It is rather that the word "sacrament" was used at an earlier time with various, less precise senses; then, as theology became more developed and precise, it became clear that there were in the Church's life seven acts which had certain essential characteristics in common with each other and were different in kind from anything else which she does, and the word became specialized to mean only these. "Sacrament" is the Western, Latin word for what we should call "mystery" if we had continued to use the Greek which was the Church's first generally used language. These things are the Church's mysteries; this, though of course connected with it, does not mean precisely what we generally use the word "mystery" for today—a doctrine which goes beyond the reach of reason, such as the doctrine of the Trinity. The Church's mysteries meant those acts of the Church in which God is in a special way mysteriously present and active. Centuries of thought were needed before Christians were clearly aware of just which of the Church's acts were, in a way common to all of them and to nothing else, mysteries of God's presence in this sense; sacraments, to use the Western term.

The final clarification took place, in the West (that is to say, in the Catholic Church from which the Eastern Orthodox were by now unhappily separated),[1] in the scholastic period of theology: that is to say, in the period, beginning from the twelfth century, when a new kind of systematic thought and writing was applied to theology and a great work of classification, arrangement and what might be called tidying-up took place. One of the influences which brought this systematization about was the application to theology of various classifications and technical terms borrowed from ancient philosophy, especially that of Aristotle. Amongst these was the distinction between matter and form, and this was applied to the sacraments.

"Matter" here does not mean precisely the same as matter the opposite of spirit, the stuff which occupies space. Roughly, in this distinction between matter and form, matter is that in anything which might equally well be either this thing or other things: wood might be shaped into any number of things; the stuff in our bodies might be the stuff of some other

[1] Although the development of sacramental doctrine was by no means complete at the time when East and West became estranged from each other, the Eastern Orthodox are in full agreement with Catholics about the meaning and number of the sacraments; the doctrinal development was simply a clarification of what was already the common doctrine of the Church.

2*

animal or of the ground under our feet; dipping in water might be a hygienic, a playful or a religious act. Form, on the other hand, is that by which this thing is itself; the wood which might have been a toast-rack is given the form of a spoon; chemicals which might have been an alligator have here the form of a human being; a particular dipping in water is given the form of Christian baptism. Matter is potentially all kinds of things; form determines it to something definite.

The sacraments do not all fit equally readily into this formula. We find we have to distinguish between "remote" and "proximate" matter; water is the remote matter of baptism, washing in water the proximate matter. The proximate matter is already to some degree determined, "formed", in contrast with the remote matter; water, on its own, might equally well be a geographical feature, a drink, an ornamental cascade, a source of hydro-electric power, etc. Here it is in fact being a bath, or at least a wash. But a wash itself can be quite a number of things, and what determines it to be Christian baptism is the form, the saying of the words commanded by Christ, with the intention (always necessary to a sacrament) that they shall have their Christian meaning.

The matter of confirmation is laying-on of

hands of a bishop or specially authorized priest, together with anointing with chrism (the anointing was almost certainly added by the Church's authority, the original gesture being only the imposition of hands). The gesture is given its Christian sacramental meaning by the accompanying words.

The matter of the Eucharist is wheaten bread and grape wine; the form, the words of consecration spoken by a priest.

The matter of penance is, remotely, the penitent's sins; proximately, it is his acts repenting, confessing and making reparation for them. The form is the absolution given by a priest authorized by the bishop. (The matter, one sees, can be as "immaterial" as the form; in another sense, both are always material, since the spoken word is necessarily part of the material world.)

The matter of the anointing of the sick is expressed in its name; it is done with oil which has been blessed by a bishop. The accompanying prayers of the priest are the form.

The matter of holy orders is the imposition of the bishop's hands; the form, the words in which he expressly prays that this man, or these men, be given the priesthood.

To apply the matter-form distinction to marriage, we are reduced to saying that in so far as one party plights his or her troth, that is the matter, but in so far as he or she accepts the plighted troth of the other, that is the form.

We may not feel that the distinction is always a great assistance in thinking about the sacraments; but it will become an actual source of confusion only if we think that the distinction between the matter and the form is the same as the distinction, essential to the sacraments, between the outward sign, belonging to our natural order, and the effect of grace, belonging to the supernatural order. On the contrary, the *matter and form together* are the outward sign, belonging to our natural world; we can speak of a sign only when an object or a gesture is "formed" to a particular meaning. In the sacraments, the sign thus consisting of "matter" and "form" does not only speak to us symbolically of a supernatural grace: by God's power, it actually causes that grace in us. The sacraments are signs which effect what they signify.

5. THE SEVEN SACRAMENTS (2)

The sacraments are signs which effect what they signify; they do not only mean something to the mind, but by meaning that something they make it real. This is because they are

Christ's own signs, sharing in the power to give supernatural life which his own body has, in its whole extended existence of life, death, resurrection, ascension and mystical continuation in the Church, leading up to his second coming.

So, by their very constitution, which is from Christ and rooted in Christ, the sacraments have the power to communicate divine life. But does this mean that they always, unfailingly, do so, regardless of the character of the minister, the manner in which they are performed, and the spirit in which they are received? Catholics in general, and many others as well, are familiar with the teaching that the unworthiness of the minister does not prevent the work of the sacrament, so long as he is someone who has authority to administer it, and means to do so; and that unseemliness, dullness, haste or any such thing in the performance of the rite does not destroy it, so long as the bare necessities of action and words remain; but that the disposition of the person receiving the sacrament does make a difference, so that, if he is sufficiently unworthy, he will be not merely failing to receive grace, but adding sacrilege to his other sins.

But this very fact, that guilty reception is sacrilege, shows that when the person receiving a sacrament frustrates, by his sin, the sacrament's grace-giving effect, he does not reduce it to nothing, or to a mere empty ceremony. The reason why an unworthy reception is not merely a waste of time but a sin of sacrilege is that a sacrament does always accomplish a real effect in the supernatural order, regardless of the dispositions of the recipient. It is the fact that he is, so to say, laying hold on that supernatural reality, in such a way as to misuse it, that makes his reception of the sacrament sacrilegious.

We find, then, that we must see three levels of action in each of the sacraments, as we go deeper into their manner of working and their effects; and the same period of scholastic theology which made the more superficial analysis into matter and form gave us also, especially on the part of St. Thomas Aquinas, deeply illuminating insight into this three-fold depth. We can see the three levels as (1) the outward sign—the actions and words performed by a duly authorized minister who really means to perform them; (2) the supernatural reality which that sign *always* achieves, no matter what guilty obstacle the recipient puts in the way; and (3) the giving of God's grace, which is received always when, but only when, the recipient does not prevent it by his bad dispositions. The names given to these three levels in scholastic theology are (1) *sacramentum tantum*, "just sacrament"—the bare sign; (2) *res et sacramentum*, reality-and-sacrament in one—a supernatural reality which is at the same time a mysterious sign; and (3) *res tantum*, sheer reality, which is union by grace with God and which is what all the sacraments are for.

Whenever we have the bare sign, the *sacramentum tantum*, validly performed, then we always have the supernatural reality, *res et sacramentum*. But we may have these two without their proper, final effect, *res tantum*, divine grace, because the person receiving the sacrament may himself frustrate its effect. And, on the other hand, that final reality, God's grace, may be given by him without the performance of the sacrament, for while we are bound to make full use of the sacraments he has given us, he is in no way bound to restrict his merciful action to their use. Thus a person may be "christened", made one with Christ, by baptism of desire, or a penitent restored to grace without sacramental absolution; or a loving Protestant, deprived by historical forces of the valid Eucharist, may be raised to a higher degree of personal union with the Blessed

Trinity than many a Catholic daily communicant.

If we look at the "bare sign", *sacramentum tantum*, in each sacrament, we can see that this is the aspect of it which any observer, however unbelieving, could see, and agree to our description of it. He might think that the whole thing was meaningless and could have no useful effect, but, given that he knows the official status of the people involved and what they are saying (even this would not always be necessary), he could see that we have, in baptism, a washing; in confirmation, an official approval, amounting to some sort of commissioning; in the Eucharist, a meal; in penance, a kind of trial and judgement; in anointing of the sick, a sort of treatment, in the medical sense, applied to the patient; in holy orders, a definite commissioning of officials; and in marriage, a contract. He might not believe that any of these things is the slightest use, or in any way effective—even the marriage contract. But, however unbelieving, he could see that these are the things which these people are doing, for whatever they are worth.

What they are worth, infallibly and certainly, is the *res et sacramentum*, the reality which they signify and which is itself significant.

The washing of baptism makes a person, not physically clean, but fundamentally new. For better or worse, a person who is baptized, even if undergoing it hypocritically for social reasons, say, is reborn as a member of the Church, which is Christ's body. The commissioning of confirmation makes a person, even if he has already ceased to believe and is merely "going through with it" to avoid fuss, an official witness of the Gospel in the body of Christ. The eucharistic meal is always, however sacrilegiously sinful the consecrating priest or communicants may be, the true body and blood of Christ.

Penance is a different case (and here the division into matter and form is very helpful). For the acts of the penitent, *including repentance*, are the matter of the sacrament; so that where there is no true repentance, there is no sacrament at all. Nevertheless, even here we have, in its own kind, the constant, indestructible element to be found in the other sacraments. The absolution of the penitent, even if he is a hypocrite in his confession and no true penitent, does give him, outwardly, an official reconciliation with the Christian community, the body of Christ.

The anointing of a sick person dedicates him, in his sickness, to God, even if it means nothing to the patient himself. If a man received holy orders in a state of mortal sin, he would have added sin to sin, but he would still be indeed a priest; and similarly, if a person contracted marriage in a state of mortal sin, that would be a sacrilege, but he or she would still be truly a husband or wife.

One consequence of this inability of even the guiltiest reception to frustrate the central, supernatural effect of the sacrament is that a later repentance can waken the sacrament to grace-giving life. The essential sacramental reality is already there, ready to achieve its full divine effect if only the person whose will is frustrating it will cease to do so. Someone who was baptized without true faith and repentance, if he is later genuinely converted, does not need to be baptized again. He has already been reborn into the body of Christ; his lack of repentance, acting as a hindrance, caused him to be, as it were, still-born; but now his repentance has wakened him to supernatural life, and he can go on to enjoy the consequences of his baptismal rebirth without any rebaptism. Similarly, if a person repents of the guilt which spiritually ruined his confirmation day, or ordination or wedding day, he will thereupon begin to enjoy the grace flowing from those sacraments. A sick person who grudgingly sub-

mits to anointing may later repent and receive
the benefit of the anointing. Penance and the
Eucharist are different, as has been said already
in the case of penance. In the Eucharist, the
res et sacramentum, the infallibly achieved
effect, is not a new status or condition in the
recipient, but a new reality under the signs of
the bread and wine: the Real Presence. Sin
does not make it less real or repentance more
real. Here, what repentance will lead to is a
right use of the sacrament in the future, making reparation for wrong use of it in the past.

In three of the sacraments, baptism, confirmation and holy orders, the supernatural
reality which is infallibly achieved by the sign
changes the person receiving the sacrament in
such a definite way that the effect can never be
undone and never repeated. There is always
something in the sacramental effect which can
never be repeated. The same bread and wine
cannot be consecrated twice, the same sin cannot be remitted twice, the same sickness cannot
be twice dedicated to God (though a relapse can
be regarded as a distinct illness) and the same
marriage cannot twice be contracted. The difference in baptism, confirmation and orders is
that this unrepeatable effect applies directly to
the *person* who receives the sacrament. He is
changed, irrevocably. You cannot be born twice

as a member of the human race; nor can you be born twice a member of Christ's body. Again, the change from child to adult is a definite physical change which can neither be reversed nor repeated; this provides a parallel to the changes in a Christian whereby he becomes, once for all, a witness to the Gospel by confirmation or a sacrificing, authority-bearing priest by holy orders.

St. Thomas tells us to see all three of these irrevocable "sealing" or "character-bearing" sacraments as an entry into Christ's priesthood. We are already members of Christ the Priest by baptism, sharing in the worship which his body, the Church, offers to God. By becoming official witnesses of that body, in confirmation, we have a fuller share in its priestly worship. And finally, those who are "ordered" to the sacrificing priesthood, especially those who, as bishops, exercise the priesthood in its fullness, share in a still further sense in the one priesthood of Christ.

We have seen now how this power of the sacramental sign to effect a sacramental reality (the "seal" in baptism, confirmation and holy orders, something equally objective in the others) means that even the wrong approach of the recipient, though it can prevent the receiving of grace, cannot make the sacrament powerless. It is easy to see that this same objective accomplishment of a supernatural reality makes the sacraments even more independent of two other "hindrances"—unworthy performance and unworthy ministers.

I began the discussion of the sacraments by insisting that they do not work *merely* at the psychological level, as powerful symbols affecting the mind in all its depths. But this does not mean that they are *not* powerful symbols in that sense. They are indeed, and baptism and the Eucharist especially. This means that it is in the highest degree desirable that they should be enacted in such a way that their tremendous symbolism comes home to the mind. Baptism ought to look and feel like a rebirth from the womb of the waters, with all the Church's additional ceremonies of solemn entrance, exorcism and anointing, the light carried in expectation of Christ, the white robe of the feast, reinforcing and underlining its meaning. The Eucharist ought to look and feel like a sacrificial meal in which all Christ's members are joined in his offering, and at his table in our Father's house. Baptism ought not to be an unintelligible muttering in a lost corner of the church, in which at one stage a little water is splashed, at another a white cloth flops for a moment onto the baby's shoulder, at another a candle is lit and blown out, without any of its seeming to mean much to anyone there. The Eucharist ought not to be reduced to a remote and inaudible ritual performed by one man at an altar while others kneel afar off in silent and lonely worship or distraction, after which such of them as have a private devotion to the practice of Communion may come up for their individual union with the Lord, unrelated to each other or to the sacrifice. It is highly desirable that the sacraments should not be reduced to any such thing, and that they should do all for men's minds that powerful symbols can do. But *they are still themselves, however badly they are done.*

However much we may wish that the Church's symbolic actions be given their full value (and it is not at all an unimportant extra, it is a question of the christianizing of the depths of Christian minds), nevertheless, the most important thing of all is that so long as the bare essentials remain (the washing in the name of the Trinity, the consecration with Christ's words of the bread and wine), we have the supernatural realities with all their power to give grace to anyone who does not impede it.

We may note here that, while the general practice of administering the sacraments in somewhat "diminished" form comes rather late in the Church's history, the recognition that they *could* be cut down to a bare minimum rite, and still be themselves, goes back to the primitive Church. The document called the *Didache* belongs to a time (second century, perhaps even first) when it was normal for baptism to be administered with the full-scale symbolism of stripping naked and going down into the waters; but it gives directions for performing baptism, if need be, just by pouring a little water over the head (as is normally done today). To take another example, Communion under both kinds was normal in the West even till the thirteenth century; but the practice of Communion under one kind for the sick, for prisoners, and for the faithful who were allowed to take the Eucharist to their homes, was already in existence in the second century at latest. The first Christians had the same view of the sacraments as we have; there might be a better or worse way of performing the rite, a fuller or a more diminished form, but the objective reality was the same.

It is perfectly reasonable that, on the other hand, sects such as the Baptists, who do not believe that baptism actually does anything in the supernatural order, should attach great importance to the way in which the rite is performed—insisting, for instance, on immersion. For to them the psychological effect of the symbol is the only effect present, so obviously there is little point in the ceremony unless it is given its maximum symbolic value. We can realize the desirability of having symbols at their strongest, but for us everything does not depend on them. Even a minimum rite can accomplish a truly supernatural end, so long as its meaning is the meaning of the sacrament. But only a maximum rite will do for a merely psychological end.

Just as a somewhat dreary and meagre performance of the rite does not prevent it from having its effect, so the power of the sacrament is also independent of the unworthiness of the minister. It is not only his personal spiritual state which, in this sense, does not matter (which is obvious enough, since he is of course not communicating his own spiritual riches but is simply a means of communicating the riches of Christ, by Christ's power and not his own); but even his relationship of communion with the one true Church does not affect his power to give a valid sacrament. Anyone whatsoever, whether baptized or not, can validly baptize. Any baptized person, however severed in belief or obedience from the Catholic Church, can confer the sacrament of marriage, given that he is free to marry. Anyone who has been validly consecrated a bishop, even though he may be in schism or heresy, can make true priests, and those he ordains can truly consecrate bread and wine to the body and blood of Christ. This is one of the things that can be most puzzling about the sacraments; for they are, essentially, acts of the Church, of the body of Christ, communicating the life of that body. How, then, can they be truly present where those who perform them are out of communion with the Church? The Church is the society of the sacraments; the sacraments belong in her; how can they be outside?

It is a question which aroused controversy at a very early date, when St. Cyprian of Carthage in the third century insisted that heretics ought to be rebaptized when reconciled to the Church. But in spite of his and a few other dissentient voices, the Church has stuck firmly to the principle that the sacraments of heretics and schismatics are valid, given the basic qualification of the minister. This means that we must see the Church as acting (for the sacraments are always her acts) through separated ministers. But the result is not "separated sacraments". Wherever a valid sacrament is administered, though it be by a heretic, there the Church is performing *her* sacrament, and that sacrament is part of the life of the Catholic Church. Thus anyone who is validly baptized is baptized into membership of the Catholic Church. If a separation from the Church takes place, it must come later, and by his own act; baptism, by whomever administered, could not make him a member of anything except the one body of Christ of which every valid baptism is an action.

But while neither sinfulness nor schism nor heresy disqualifies a person from conferring a valid sacrament, there does remain something by which the minister may prevent the sacrament from being itself. The sacrament will still be valid even if the minister perform it in a very unseemly, slipshod way, but the bare essentials of the sign must remain. This means that both the action, such as the washing, must remain, and also its meaning, as expressed in the appropriate words spoken by the minister of the sacrament and so intended by him. The person conferring a sacrament must mean it to be the Christian rite which it represents: without that intention, there is no sacrament. This does not mean only that a wedding performed in a film, say, would not bind the two actors together for life. It also means that a definite intention to make the rite have some other meaning, exclusive of its actual meaning in the life of the Church, would destroy it as a sacrament.

For example: If a person who held that baptism does not give spiritual rebirth, but is only a symbolic expression of it, were to baptize people with the definite intention of not giving them rebirth through the sacrament, then his lack of a real sacramental intention would have destroyed the sacrament; he would have made the rite into something else, not Christian baptism. It would be all the clearer if, to express his intention, he altered the words from "I baptize thee in the name of the Father and of the Son and of the Holy Ghost" to, for example, "I baptize thee in the name of the Lord Jesus." It is not that this second form (which may possibly have been sometimes used by the early Christians) does of itself exclude the doctrine of rebirth. But if he chose it because the traditional formula is associated with the traditional belief, and he wanted to express his rejection of the traditional belief, then he would be, by a change of form which expressed a change of intention, destroying the nature of the sacrament.

Again: If two people went through a form of marriage intending that it should be, not a lifelong and unbreakable union, but a temporary one, which they could end if they chose, then that would be no marriage and hence no sacrament. They might make their intention clear by cutting out the "for better, for worse ... till death" phrases from the marriage service. It is not that the simple statement "I take thee for my wife" (or "husband") is necessarily insufficient to express true marriage: it could perfectly well express it, if the permanence were taken for granted, as it should be. But if those phrases, normally present, were deliberately cut out, this would indicate a change in the meaning of the rite thus administered, so that it would no longer be the rite, and Christian sacrament, of marriage.

It was because of an alteration in intention of this kind that the Pope, Leo XIII, in the Bull *Apostolicae Curae*, judged that the orders administered in the Church of England are not true priestly orders. There was, at the time of the Reformation, an alteration by Protestants in the meaning of the priesthood, excluding from it the sacrificial power which is as essential to it as rebirth to baptism or permanence to marriage; and this alteration was intentionally embodied in the Anglican liturgy and rite of ordination. Hence the Church can only regard those who have received that rite as having received something other than the Catholic priesthood, since the rite was drawn up to exclude something which is essential to the Catholic priesthood.

The question at issue over Anglican Orders is not whether the Church of England is a part of the Catholic Church; for the corporate Catholic institution, the Church in England, which Elizabeth I inherited in 1559, was in any case suppressed by her when she ousted and replaced all its bishops. The religious institution with which she replaced it was, clearly enough by the mere fact of replacement, a new institution and not the Catholic Church; but the question could still arise whether valid sacraments (besides baptism and marriage, which did indeed continue) might have been introduced into this new society by real, though heretical and schismatical, bishops. To this question Rome has given the answer "No", on the basis of the Church's sacramental doctrine concerning intention in the sacraments and the form which expresses it. Discussion of the matter is apt to be profitless, and a distraction from the real issue between Anglicans and Catholics, which is the nature of the Church and her unity; but it seemed necessary to say something about it in connection with the wider truth that valid sacraments *can* (so long as the intention is not falsified) continue amongst heretics and schismatics.

6. THE SEVEN SACRAMENTS (3)

It will be useful now to remember the catechism definition of a sacrament as "an outward sign of inward grace, ordained by Jesus Christ, by which grace is given to our souls". The first and last part of this definition would not tell us enough, if we had nothing more to go on, because they do not unite the outward sign and the inward grace closely enough. We could say that a sacramental such as holy water, or a pilgrimage, was an outward sign of inward grace by which grace was given to our souls; but we should be using the words in a different sense. We need to realize that in the case of the sacraments even the simple word "by" means something unique. Grace is given to us by many means; the power which the sacraments have to give it is unique, and is summed up in the statement that the sacraments are signs which effect what they signify. And it is because they are Christ's own signs that they have this power of actually making real the thing which they outwardly mean. The three elements in the catechism definition are not three separate elements, as though you might have some ceremony to which two of them applied, but this wouldn't be a sacrament because the third one was missing. In the sense in which these phrases apply to the sacraments, they are all dependent on each other and none of them could apply to anything else. They are signs of grace by which the grace of which they are signs is actually produced, and this is simply because they are Christ's signs of Christ's grace.

The sacraments are Christ's signs, "ordained by Jesus Christ". In the case of some of them—baptism, the Eucharist, penance—we can point to a definite occasion of "institution". In others we cannot, or not with the same certainty. This does not, of course, present us with any grave difficulty; our Lord said many things to the Apostles which are not explicitly recorded in the Gospels, and it would be perfectly easy to suppose that he gave definite instructions about all the sacraments during that time between his resurrection and ascension which he spent with them "speaking of the Kingdom of God". But in considering the meaning of the phrase "ordained by Jesus Christ", it would be a mistake to think that we were considering something in the sacraments which in some cases we know explicitly in the Gospel, but of which in others we have no scriptural knowledge at all, being sure of it simply on the tradition of the Church. The division is not so clear-cut, for there is a wider and a narrower sense in which we can speak of our Lord's institution of the sacraments, and in its wider sense we can see it in the Gospels for all the sacraments. In the wider sense, our Lord was engaged in *making* the sacraments throughout his ministry and indeed throughout his life. To take it at its most obvious, he was making the Eucharist in his sermon after feeding the five thousand and, supremely, in his actual physical death on Calvary, as well as at the moment at the Last Supper when he gave the words of consecration and the command "Do this in memory of me." We can look both at the wider making and at the particular moment of institution: they are both Christ "ordaining" the sacrament. Now, for all seven we can see the wider making of the sacrament by Christ, as we shall see in the separate chapters on the sacraments: it is only that for some of them we do, and for some we do not, have a record of the narrower, particular moment of command which can be called the institution.

As Christ's signs the sacraments are, as has been said already, a uniting of us at three levels to Christ. They look to the past; Christ, the cause of our salvation, in his life, death, resurrection and ascension, is acting in them. They look to the present; Christ in his body the Church is by them uniting us by grace with the Blessed Trinity; and they look to the future, preparing us for the second coming of Christ in glory. They are thus building up the body of Christ towards its final completion in the fulfilment of all history. And as the final perfection of the body of Christ is the goal towards which all the sacraments are building up, so here and now the sacramental body of Christ, the Eucharist, is the goal to which all the other six sacraments are building up. Baptism and confirmation make a person first a member, then a fully responsible member of the community which offers, feeds on and is united in the Eucharist; penance restores us to that communion if we destroy our right to it; anointing of the sick either restores a person, by his recovery, to active membership of that communion again, or prepares him for death, a preparation completed and sealed by Viaticum; marriage is designed for the fostering of new members of the eucharistic community; orders gives men the power to offer the eucharistic sacrifice, in which Christ's members join by feeding upon him. The Eucharist is the goal and culmination of the sacraments, and to help me to bring this out in what follows I am even going to depart from the traditional order of treating the sacraments.

The traditional order is to speak first of the three sacraments of initiation into the body of

Christ: baptism, which begins it, confirmation, which seals it, and the Eucharist, which is its consummation. Then come the two sacraments of restoration and healing, penance and anointing; and lastly the two sacraments for the social building up of the body, orders and marriage. Because I want to stress the Eucharist as the goal and climax, I am going to write of it last; and because of this change I am also going to treat of marriage before holy orders, because it seems fitting to place together the sacrament of those who directly serve the altar and the Sacrament of the Altar itself.

PART II

1. BAPTISM

Christ made the sacraments; not only at some one brief moment when he instituted each by a direct command, but in a process of many acts, culminating in the sacrificial death, resurrection and ascension in which he united men with God and because of which the Holy Spirit is poured forth upon mankind. In all the sacraments we can see this work of making; and we can see, in each of them, a relationship to the saving power of Christ's passover, his passing from natural life, through death, into glorified life. In none of them is it clearer than in baptism.

Baptism is the rite of rebirth. In Christ, the New Adam, the human race was reborn, and this regeneration was finally achieved in his death and resurrection. In baptism, we are made one with him in his death and resurrection in such a way that this rebirth is applied to us; we are reborn into a new life in him. In order to understand as fully as we can why this rebirth should have been given to us in the form of baptism, we need to look first at the natural meaning of the sign which has been made into this sacrament, then at the way in which God's revelation charged it with still more meaning during the preparatory age of the Old Testament, and finally at what Christ himself has done with it. This is true of all the sacraments; when Christ gave us these signs with their completely new sacramental power, the materials which he took for them were already rich with meaning from the use that God had long been making of them, as types and foreshadowings: and behind the Old Testament types, in turn, lies the common stuff of symbolism which is part of man's very nature.

In plain fact, and before we come to anything symbolic, water does dissolve material things; in particular, it washes off dirt; it is, in the highest probability, the environment in which living beings first existed, from which they came forth; and if, in accordance with common usage, we apply the word "water" to the fluid in the womb, each one of us came forth from it into this world. At the same time, we cannot live in it for any length of time; if we try to, we drown. It is not surprising, then, that both in myth and in the depths of individual minds water should be the symbol both of death and of coming into life. To go down into the waters means to go down into darkness, death, shapeless chaos, where all is dissolved: but to come up out of the waters means to be renewed in fresh life and vigour: indeed, it is just because the waters will swallow up and dissolve our old, tired, worn-out life that they can bring forth fresh, strong, new life. This image is not peculiar to Christianity: it is widespread and deep in the mind of man.[1]

This primary meaning of the waters is caught up and enriched in the revelation of the Old Testament. Here too, as in many of the creation myths of the pagans, we are shown the chaos of waters as the source out of which the world of forms comes forth. But here, in Gen. 1.2, the vision is of the Spirit of God brooding over the waters, and calling the world of forms out of them by his Word. In the Easter Vigil, as one of the readings which are a preparation for the blessing of the baptismal water, the Church evokes this image before our minds; the Spirit of God calling creation out of the primeval waters, as he calls the new creation out of the waters of baptism.

Then, in the story of Noe, we have the inspired form of another widespread image: the swallowing up of the world of forms in the

[1] See Mircea Eliade, *Patterns in Comparative Religion*, London, Sheed and Ward, 1958, Chapter 5, "The Waters and Water Symbolism"; and L. Beirnaert, S.J., "The Mythical Dimension in Christian Baptism", in *Selection I*, London, Sheed and Ward, 1951.

waters once again, so that what had been created was dissolved, but a nucleus of life, human and animal, was preserved, so that life came forth renewed from the Flood. In the Bible form of the story the emphasis is on sin as the reason for the Flood; it is not just the world but the *sinful* world that is swallowed up and dissolved, and not just life but righteous, virtuous life that is preserved to be a new beginning. In the New Testament itself, in the First Epistle of St. Peter (3.20–1), we are told to see this as an image of baptism, in which sin is washed away and from which righteous life comes forth.

But something new is introduced by God into the meaning of the waters when we come to the Exodus. Here we step out of the world of general symbolism, common to many myths and religions, into the world which is special to the Jewish revelation whose climax is Jesus Christ. Here we have the revelation of the God who acts in history, who intervenes in the world of national and international events to rescue his chosen people from slavery in Egypt, taking them safely through the waters of the Red Sea on their first stage towards the Promised Land. This was the decisive event which made Israel God's people: the most important single event in history until the coming of Christ. And we are bidden, first by St. Paul (1 Cor.

10.1–2), then by a chorus of the Fathers, and by the liturgy of the Church in the Easter Vigil, to see our baptism as the fulfilment of the prefiguring type which that tremendous rescue was. We pass through the waters in safety, as Israel did; sin and the devil are swallowed up in them behind us, like Pharaoh's pursuing army; thus we become God's own people, and begin our march towards the eternal Promised Land.

Further enrichment of the symbol with even more of the meaning that it is to bear in baptism is given in some of the prophecies belonging to a later age of Israel's history. A constant theme of the Prophets is that of restoration; devastating punishment first, the punishment of national destruction and deportation for the people's endless sins, but afterwards a glorious restoration, even more glorious than what went before. It is especially through these prophecies of even *more* glorious restoration that we can see the ultimate meaning of prophecy, Christ's reign of grace, shining through the immediate meaning of the return from captivity. It is when the prophet foretells a *new thing* that we can know that he is, ultimately, speaking of the new creation. And over and over again, as we should expect, we find this theme of the new creation coming through the symbol of purifying, even though sometimes terrifying, waters; preparing for the rebirth in Christ's new creation which will be by the waters of baptism.

Thus Isaias says (Chapter 4)—and again the Church reads it to us at the Easter Vigil—"The Lord shall wash away the filth of the daughters of Sion, and shall wash away the blood of Jerusalem out of the midst thereof, by the spirit of judgement and by the spirit of burning. And the Lord will create upon every place of Mount Sion, and where he is called upon, a cloud by day and a smoke and the brightness of a flaming fire in the night: for over all the glory shall be a protection." The wonders of the Exodus, water and cloud and fire, are to be renewed still more wonderfully.

By the mouth of Jeremias (Chapter 31) God promises: "I will bring them through the torrents of waters in a right way, and they shall not stumble . . . Behold the days shall come, and I will make a *new* covenant with the house of Israel . . . I will give my law in their bowels, and I will write it in their heart: and I will be their God, and they shall be my people. And they shall teach no more every man his neighbour, and every man his brother, saying: Know the Lord: for all shall know me from the least even to the greatest."

Perhaps the richest of all are the prophecies of Ezechiel, which we have in the liturgy of paschal time. "I will pour upon you clean water, and you shall be cleansed from all your filthiness ... And I will give you a new heart, and put a new spirit within you: and I will take away the stony heart out of your flesh, and will give you a heart of flesh. And I will put my spirit in the midst of you: and I will cause you to walk in my commandments, and to keep my judgements, and do them." (36.25–7.) In Chapter 47 we have the vision of an unfordable torrent of waters pouring from the resurrected Temple, bringing life wherever it flows.

Thus when Christ our Lord began to fashion the sacramental sign of baptism by water, his raw material, so to speak, was not simply water as everywhere deeply significant to man, but the water over which God's Spirit brooded in creation; water in which a sinful world had been washed away and a new, righteous world begun; water through which God's people had passed to safety in that most tremendous act of their history, the Exodus; water through whose symbolism the Prophets had glimpsed the vision of a new order, a new creation of grace.

Christ's making of the sacrament began with his very entry into the world; for from early times the Church has seen Mary's womb as a type of the baptismal font. As the Virgin was made fruitful by the Spirit to bring forth the

3*

New Adam, so the virginal waters are made fruitful by the Spirit to bring forth children of the new creation: the font is the womb of Mother Church, bearing divine life as Mary bore the source of divine life.

The beginning of the plain and literal making of the sacrament of baptism is of course Christ's own baptism in the Jordan, the starting point of his public life. The making of Christian baptism spans the whole course of that life, which began with his sanctification of the visible sign by his own submission to it and ended with the death and resurrection by which he gave that sign a spiritual power which of itself it could not have.

John's baptism was a baptism of water only, not of water and the Spirit. It was salutary and pleasing to God in so far as it expressed, by an appropriate sign, the repentance for which John called in his preaching. It could have a spiritual effect simply in the same way as any other ritual washing, if done with a sincere intention, expressing the will to repentance and purity; such washings as were practised, for instance, by communities of devout Jews of the type that lived at Qumran on the Dead Sea. John's preaching and baptism had, indeed, a worth which no other had, because his was God's own last message of preparation to his people; John was the last of the Old Testament

prophets. But his baptism was a sign of repentance only; not an effective sign truly giving the
grace it signified.

It was this sign, "empty" in this sense, which
Jesus sanctified by himself submitting to it.
The inappropriateness of baptizing him, who
needed no repentance and is the source of all
grace, immediately struck his cousin, the Baptist (Matt. 3.14). Our Lord, however, insisted
on doing publicly what it was right and necessary for others to do; but where others received,
he gave. He went down into the waters of chaos
and dissolution, but not in weakness, submitting to their symbolic destructive and recreative power. He descended into them in
conquering strength to give them his own
recreative power: we can see his baptism as
sanctifying all the waters of the world, trans-
forming the natural element into the material
of sacrament. The voice from heaven at his
baptism—"This is my beloved son, in whom
I am well pleased"—proclaims what he is in
himself, not what his baptism made him. But
it also proclaims what our baptism makes us,
in him: sons in the Son. He already possessed
fully the Holy Spirit, who that day visibly
descended upon him in the form of a dove;
whereas we, in our baptism, really receive the
Spirit.

Already, then, in his own baptism, Christ

gave to the outward sign its inward sacramental meaning; but its power to make real that meaning was to come from his death and resurrection, so Christian baptism was not yet in being. Hence St. John tells us that though the Apostles continued, in the way of John the Baptist, to baptize as the appropriate sign of repentance, Jesus himself did not baptize. (John 4.2.) He had not completed the making of the sacrament; the completion of the making of all the sacraments is his final passover through death to glory, of which the passage of the Red Sea was a type.

In the meanwhile, he gave his teaching on what baptism was to be. John had already foretold that the One who was to come would baptize with the Holy Spirit. (Matt. 3.11.) Jesus teaches Nicodemus (John 3) that to enter into God's kingdom one must be born again: for what is born of the flesh is flesh, and what is born of the spirit is spirit. Our natural birth gives us natural life, with both material and (in the human sense) spiritual powers, but it is all "flesh" in the New Testament sense: mere human nature. If we are to be "spirit" in the New Testament sense—sharers in divine life— then we must be born again of the Spirit; and our Lord here already proclaims that the manner of it is to be "of water and the Spirit". The power of the sign of water to accomplish this is to be supplied by himself, by a baptism of which his baptism in Jordan was only a symbol. Could his disciples, so eager to share his glory, bear to share in that terrible baptism, he asks them? (Mark 10.38.) But, terrible though it is, for it is his passion and death, he longs for it, crying out that "I have a baptism wherewith I am to be baptized, and how am I straitened until it be accomplished!" (Luke 12.50.) By that baptism, giving its inner meaning to the sign which he has already sanctified, sins will be washed away: and so all his individual pardonings of sin are an anticipation of it; Satan will be vanquished: and so all his castings-out of devils look forward to it; and above all, the whole creation will be made new, so that in this rebirth men can come to share again in the life of God which was lost at the Fall, the life of which Christ speaks, under the symbol of living water, in the fourth and seventh chapters of St. John's gospel.

In that final baptism, he does in reality what his descent into Jordan symbolized. Then, he went down into the waters which symbolize death and destruction. Now, he goes down in truth into death and destruction. But now, as then, he goes down in triumphant strength. Death cannot defeat him: it is death which is defeated. Christ rises triumphant in new and glorious life, takes that glorious life into the presence of the Father and, in virtue of the union between God and mankind which he has thus accomplished, sends the Holy Spirit upon the Church. Only then, when the Spirit is given, is the making of baptism complete: the descent of the Spirit upon them, Jesus told the Apostles (Acts 1.5), would be their final baptism. Hence it is not till after Pentecost that they are to start carrying out the command which he laid upon them on the mountain in Galilee after the Resurrection: the command to go and make disciples of all nations, baptizing them in the name of the Father and of the Son and of the Holy Ghost (Matt. 28.19; cf. Mark 16.15–16), which we can call the actual institution of the sacrament of baptism.

In baptism, then, symbolized by the flowing of water from Christ's side on the Cross, his redemptive passover is present, in action, as rebirth; washing away sins, casting out the devil, and giving a new, supernatural life as a member of Christ's body, thus restoring the grace lost by Adam, the grace whose absence in us at birth is what we mean by original sin. Whenever the rite is correctly and intentionally performed even by an unbeliever, whether on a believing adult, an unconscious baby, a person with erroneous misunderstanding of the Faith, or even a person insincerely submitting for some non-religious motive,[1] then there takes place this rebirth into a new order of life in Christ's body, producing an irrevocable change ("character" or "seal") in the person baptized. This rebirth by indentification with Christ in his death and resurrection is, as we have seen earlier, what is called the *res et sacramentum*, the sign-and-reality combined, in this sacrament. It is accomplished simply by the power of Christ active in his sacrament, and not by any contribution of the recipient. Hence it is truly accomplished in a baby. It is even truly accomplished in a recipient with a false motive; but in this case, it is *all* that is accomplished, for the recipient's wrong disposition sets up a barrier against the result which the sign-reality is meant to have: the *res tantum*, the sheer reality for which the sacrament exists. The baby sets up no such barrier, and so, like the adult who approaches with faith, the baby receives the full reality: and the insincere recipient too, if ever he comes to repent and believe, will receive that reality as the delayed result of the seal, the rebirth, which has already been accomplished in him. One might say that the opposition of

[1] The candidate must, however, be willing to submit to the *rite*, for whatever motive; the performance of the rite by physical force on a person physically resisting it would not be the sacrament at all.

his will caused him to be born dead; but grace can raise the dead.

The sign-reality, then, is rebirth as a member of Christ in his body, the Church. The ultimate reality for which it exists is that life above our human nature, that supernatural life, which makes us sharers in the divine nature. (2 Pet. 1.4.) It is the indwelling of the three Persons of the Trinity, present in a wholly new way in us over and above their presence in all created things, reforming the substance of our humanity so that, by their intimate action in us, we are enabled to live by divine life; to know with divine knowledge, in the darkness of faith in this life but in the light of direct vision in heaven; to hold on, by the confident longing of hope, to that future fulfilment; and to love with divine love, already in this life. It means that we are made one with the Son so that we can, in him, truly call the Father "Our Father", by the gift of the Spirit who proceeds from both.

This union is given us in the Church, which is the body of Christ: that is, through Christ's humanity, for it is as man, glorified, triumphant man, that he is Head of the Body. We are baptized into Christ; and St. Paul's teaching on baptism (Rom. 6.3–5) brings out the way in which our union with him is related to the past, the present and the future.

First, we are baptized into Christ's past redemptive action: "Know you not that all we who are baptized in Christ Jesus are baptized in his death? For we are buried together with him by baptism into death." Second, we are baptized into his present, living body on earth, in which we live in him and share in his sacrifice of his body, feeding upon that body sacramentally; baptism, like all the sacraments, is ordered to the Eucharist. St. Paul sums up this present life in Christ: ". . . that as Christ is risen from the dead by the glory of the Father, so we also may walk in newness of life." And thirdly, we are baptized for his future, glorious return, in which the Resurrection which we share sacramentally now will be accomplished literally in our own bodies: "For if we have been planted together in the likeness of his death, we shall be also in the likeness of his resurrection." By the power of what he did once for all, made present to us in the rite which he gave, we are united with Christ who was, and is, and is to come; and by that union with Christ in his humanity, God gives himself to us: the three Persons of the Trinity, by their indwelling presence, raising us to fellowship with themselves.

2. CONFIRMATION

The chief difficulty which one feels at first
sight of the sacrament of confirmation is to
think of anything that is left for it to do which
baptism has not already done. The ready
answer to "What do we receive in confirmation?" would be "The Holy Ghost", which is
entirely correct. But we already receive the
Holy Ghost in baptism. Indeed, if a person
did not believe he was in a state of grace, with
the three Persons already dwelling in him, he
would have no right to present himself for
confirmation: it would be gravely sacrilegious,
though, like insincerely received baptism, it
would be valid, its own special "seal" would
be accomplished in him and, if he subse-
quently repented, the sacrament would then
take its full effect in him.

But we have the problem, what does confirmation add to baptism, that we should regard
it as a separate sacrament? In the early
Church, it was normally conferred immediately after baptism, and it would be hard to
establish from the documents that it was always
clearly distinguished as another sacrament.
What makes it particularly hard to be clear
about this is that the rite of baptism ended, as
it still does, with an anointing of the newly
baptized person with chrism. In the early

days, the newly baptized, emerging naked from the water, would have this sacramental oil poured all over them, from head to foot; now, the anointing is represented by pouring chrism upon the head alone. This is not, and was not, the distinct sacrament of confirmation; but it does not make matters clearer that we cannot always know, when an anointing or "signing" is referred to, whether it means this anointing, which is part of the ceremony of baptism, or a different sacrament.

On the other hand, the evidence of the New Testament is very clear indeed. In Chapter 8 of the Acts of the Apostles we are told of the converts in Samaria who, after their baptism by Philip, were given the gift of the Holy Spirit by the laying-on of hands by Peter and John, who made a special visit to them for the purpose, like any modern bishop visiting a parish to administer confirmation. The same distinction is assumed in Paul's question to "certain disciples" at Ephesus (Acts 19.1–6), "Have you received the Holy Ghost since ye believed?"; though here the answer he received showed that, though he had thought differently, these men were not yet even baptized. It is quite clear, then, that the gift of the Spirit was conferred by a special laying-on of hands quite distinct from baptism (though we have, in this connection, God's very striking

demonstration of his own sovereign freedom
in dispensing his gifts independently of the
sacraments, in the manifest outpouring of the
Holy Ghost on Cornelius and his household
even before they were baptized). (Acts 10.44–8.)

There is nothing to indicate that any anointing was included at this earliest stage of the
Church's life: within the limits of the essential meaning of the sign, the Church has
authority to modify the outward rite of the
sacrament; she has, for example, authority to
require that certain particular words, not given
in Scripture, shall be used. At present, and
since very early times, the matter of confirmation is laying-on of hands together with chrism
blessed by the bishop.

But while we can clearly see in the Acts
of the Apostles, what we know from the teaching Church, that there is such a sacrament
distinct from baptism, yet we may still be
puzzled about its function. Like baptism, it
"seals" the recipient; that is, he is changed
spiritually in a definite, irrevocable way that
can never be repeated. What is this change,
beyond the change that is already accomplished in baptism?

In Part I of this book, reference was already made to the teaching of St. Thomas
Aquinas that the three "sealing" sacraments
represent deeper and deeper stages of initia-

tion into the priesthood of Christ. Somehow, a person who has been confirmed (or perhaps, whose baptism has been confirmed: this may be the right way of understanding the word) is more fully involved in Christ's worship, as perfect man, of the Father, than one who is only baptized. Together with this we have the teaching that confirmation is especially the sacrament of fortitude; of standing firm in the Faith. And the special miraculous sign which was often granted at the moment of confirmation, in the Apostolic age, was that of "speaking with tongues".

Taking it all together, we are led to see confirmation as the sacrament of *witnessing to Christ*, of proclaiming his truth to the world. In baptism, we are given all the treasures of the body of Christ to enjoy; in confirmation, we are given them to share. Not that a person who is baptized but not confirmed *cannot* show forth the Gospel and share the riches of it with others; he can and should. But confirmation gives us official, priestly commissioning as witnesses: by its seal, its *res et sacramentum*, sign-reality, we are made, once for all, witnesses; a part of the face which the Church turns outward to the world. We are official witnesses from that moment, whether we do anything about it or not; it is only open to us to be good witnesses or bad witnesses, making good use or not of the *res tantum*, the sheer reality of the sacrament, which is the gift of the Spirit.

The basic, human gesture of commissioning, vesting with a certain power to perform a task, is the raw material which Christ fashioned into this sacrament. And again, before we come to his crystallization of it, it must be seen as charged with the meaning of all such commissionings in the life of the Chosen People. The special callings of prophets, from Moses onwards; the anointings of priests and kings, which are the reason why the Church introduced an anointing into confirmation, since it gives Christians a further share in the royal priesthood of Christ's body; the setting apart of the tribe of Levi for the service of the Tabernacle—we should see all these looming behind the bishop as a succession of men and women, boys and girls, kneel before him to be anointed, signed, endowed through his hands with the Spirit for their official task of witnessing.

Our Lord's working of this "raw material" into his sacrament does not, in this case, show any of the emphasis on the sign itself which we found in baptism. The sign here is so simple and obvious that it seems hardly to need special emphasis. There is an ancient tradition that we should look upon Christ's laying of his hands upon children, to bless them, as the giving of

the sign: "Of such is the kingdom of heaven"
—and confirmation signifies a certain definite
entering into possession of that kingdom.

But we should perhaps concentrate rather
upon Christ's teaching on witnessing, and on
the giving of the Spirit. While witnessing with
the fullness of teaching authority was a task
laid directly upon the Apostles, all the members of the Church are meant to share in that
witness; this is the very meaning of the sacrament of confirmation, which is meant to be
received by all, even by infants if in danger of
death.

We all share, then, in our degree, in the task
laid on the Apostles to "make disciples of all
nations" (Matt. 28.19), to "preach the gospel
to every creature" (Mark 16.15), to "be witnesses unto me in Jerusalem, and in all Judea,
and Samaria, and even to the uttermost part
of the earth" (Acts 1.8). This is a sharing in
Christ himself, as anything sacramental must
be; a sharing in the task he declared as his
before Pilate: "For this was I born, and for
this came I into the world; that I should give
testimony to the truth." (John 18.37.) Our
share in this task involves our final relationship with Christ in his second coming: "For
he that shall be ashamed of me and my words
... the Son of Man also will be ashamed of
him, when he shall come in the glory of his

Father with the holy angels." (Mark 8.38.) But
the essential power to bear witness comes not
from ourselves but from the Spirit: "It is not
you that speak, but the Spirit of your Father
that speaketh in you." (Matt. 10.20.) Hence,
when he told the Apostles just before the
Ascension that their task was to be "witnesses
of these things", he added, "I send the promise
of my Father upon you: stay in the city, till
you be endued with power from on high."
(Luke 24.48–9.) In seeing how he made this
sacrament, like all the sacraments, by his passover, we thus find the emphasis shifted from
Calvary to Pentecost. But it is only a shift of
emphasis within the one great act. For it was
by his death and entering into glory that he
united men with God and thus sent the gift
of the Spirit upon them. "As yet the Spirit was
not given, because Jesus was not glorified",
says St. John (7.39); and our Lord tells the
Apostles, "It is expedient to you that I go: for
if I go not, the Paraclete will not come to you;
but if I go, I will send him to you." (John 16.7.)
His going from them was, first, into death, and
so into the glory of the Resurrection and at
last out of their sight in the Ascension.

The power to witness is obtained by Christ's
sacrifice; and it is the task of a witness to bear
testimony to the truth and power of that sacrifice both in its original historical form and in

its present sacramental continuation in the Eucharist; hence the office of witness is a sharing in the priesthood. Since confirmation gives this spiritually adult relationship to the Eucharist, it used to be, and it still is in the East, received before First Communion, and this is the appropriate position for it. The only reason for the present, reverse custom general amongst Catholics of the West is that a period came when *both* sacraments were postponed until adolescence. Then St. Pius X restored child Communion, but confirmation was, so to say, left behind at the unfortunately late age to which it had, with the Eucharist, been relegated. As a sealing and confirming of baptism it used to be given, in the early Church, immediately after baptism. As a conferring of the laity's full share in Christ's priesthood, it should at least come before the full sharing in the eucharistic sacrifice, which is sacramental Communion.

In confirmation, then, Christ's death and resurrection are actively present as the uniting of men with God which obtained the Spirit of Truth for men. By it we are made one with Christ the Witness, who bore witness to the truth even to death; we are made, here and now, witnesses to his body the Church in all the fullness of its life: especially its sacrificial life, for this sacrament is a sharing in Christ's priesthood, and, like all the sacraments, points to the Eucharist. Looking to the future, we are given the grace to be steadfast witnesses, if necessary even to death ("martyr" simply means "witness"), so that, when the Son of Man comes in his glory we may deserve the blessing promised in Matt. 10.32: "Every one therefore that shall confess me before men, I will also confess him before my Father who is in heaven."

3. PENANCE

Though the problem is a very different one, it would be possible to ask concerning the sacrament of penance the same question as arises over confirmation: "What possible need can there be for it, after baptism?" We could make our objection scripturally: "For it is impossible for those who were once illuminated, have tasted also the heavenly gift, and were made partakers of the Holy Ghost . . . and are fallen away: to be renewed again to penance, crucifying again to themselves the Son of God, and making him a mockery." (Heb. 6.4–6.) We remember that St. John says that "whosoever is born of God, sinneth not" (1 John 5.18), and that St. Paul expresses over and over again, in different ways, the theme "We that are dead to sin, how shall we live any longer therein?" (Rom. 6.2.)

We might get the impression from this (and many non-Catholic Christians do get it) that the Christian community, the Church, necessarily consists of people for whom, having put away the sinfulness of the old man in baptism, sin is quite unthinkable. Grave sin, that is, such as contradicts the life of God in us so that they cannot exist together; what we nowadays, perfectly accurately, call mortal sin, i.e., killing sin. We certainly do not even have to consider the possibility that all the minor human failings were absent from the first Christians. Indeed, they are very much in evidence: the uncharitable criticisms of St. Paul and his sources of income, for which he rebukes the Corinthians; the quarrelsomeness of those same Corinthians, the trouble, whatever it was, between Evodia and Synteche at Philippi, Paul's own quarrel with Barnabas, in which both, apparently, lost their tempers—the Douai translation uses much milder wording, I gather, than the Greek—in Acts 15.39; St. Peter's timid surrender to human respect at Antioch (Gal. 2.12); the selfishness of the Corinthians towards the poorer brethren, which St. Paul rebukes in 1 Cor. 11.20–2; the worldly subservience of those whom St. James reproves for honouring a rich member of the congregation and despising a poor one (2.1–6); the necessity of choosing the clergy from among men who will not be over-fond of wine, quarrelling, money or sins of the tongue (1 Tim. 3.3, 8): no-one could think of the New Testament Church for a moment as a community of people without faults, even if we suppose that nothing was ever involved in all this beyond what we should nowadays call venial sins. But what about the real turning of one's back on God, by such acts as apostasy, murder or adultery, which are simply incompatible, as St. John says, with the life which is born of God?

"It is absolutely heard that there is fornication among you, and such fornication as the like is not among the heathens; that one should have his father's wife" (1 Cor. 5.1). St. Paul is stricken with horror: we must admit that we can hardly imagine a bishop of the Church today striking just this note of appalled astonishment that fornication should exist amongst his flock. But the change is in atmosphere, the similarity is in hard fact; St. Paul's Church, like ours, was not one in which mortal sin just did not happen. Nor does one simply cease to be a member of the Church by such sin. In the next chapter of the same epistle, St. Paul points out that the real horror of fornication committed by a Christian is precisely that he is, even in his sin, a member of Christ: "Shall I then take the members of Christ and make

them the members of an harlot? God forbid."
(1 Cor. 6.15.)

This denial of one's baptism by mortal sin
was known in the Church from the beginning,
then. But the crucial question is, was there, is
there, any remedy? At first sight, the Epistle
to the Hebrews seems to say, No: you have
had the remedy, baptism, already, and it cannot be repeated. Yet St. Paul seems to hold out
some hope for the incestuous Corinthian
(1 Cor. 5.5); and St. John, a few verses before
he tells us that whoever is born of God does
not sin, tells us, "He that knoweth his brother
to sin a sin which is not to death, let him ask,
and life shall be given to him, who sinneth
not to death." (1 John 5.16.) He adds, "There
is a sin unto death: for that I say not that any
man ask." He faced the possibility of hopeless
cases, but all cases were not hopeless; it was
possible that a brother who had lost the life
of God by sin should yet have life given him.
The end of St. James' Epistle is on the same
theme. The Epistle to the Hebrews, then, is
only giving us an emphatic reminder that
baptism cannot be repeated; what is done in
us then is final, irrevocable. If we contradict
it by our sin, we cannot start all over again
with a fresh baptism: that would be a mockery.
But is baptism the Church's only means of
forgiving sins?

It is indeed her principal means. We are so apt to think of baptism as always given to babies that we get into the habit of regarding it as solely the remedy for original sin, and penance as that for personal sin. But that was not the dominating picture in the early Church, nor is it now in any part of the Church where she is breaking new ground; it is not of the essence of baptism to be a sacrament for babies, for the personally innocent. Baptism is in fact the Church's great and foremost remedy for sin. Hence, when Christian writers of the first three hundred years or so commented upon our Lord's words to the Apostles on Easter Sunday, "Whose sins you shall forgive, they are forgiven them, whose sins you shall retain, they are retained" (John 20.23), they always referred them to the sacrament of baptism. Those whom the Church admitted to baptism were, by her baptizing, forgiven their sins; those whom, after scrutiny of them and their motives, she refused to admit, were left in their sins, their sins were retained. From the fourth century onwards, we begin to find writers who apply this text both to the Church's power to baptize and to her power to absolve. For it does indeed apply to both: the Church has, and was from the beginning conscious of having, the two means of forgiveness. It is a change in emphasis that whereas Christians of the first centuries would automatically understand the text as meaning *primarily*, "Whose sins you shall forgive by baptism, they are forgiven them . . .", those of a later date, including ourselves, would think of it primarily as, "Whose sins you shall forgive by absolution, they are forgiven them." But both are included in our Lord's words, for he said "Whose sins you shall forgive, they are forgiven", without distinction; all sins are included, whether committed before or after baptism.

In fact, of course, most Christians recognize clearly enough that we do sin after baptism, and still sin, most of us, even after the kind of general repentance and turning to God which perhaps corresponds psychologically, for most of us, to the conversion and adult baptism of the first Christians. Practically everyone realizes that we can destroy the life of God within us after we have begun to live it; many of us, at least, realize that we have done so. But, in general, thank God, we do not despair. Most Christians remember the parables of the Lost Sheep and the Prodigal Son; they are confident that it is still possible for them to leave their sins and return to their Father's house. The difference between most non-Catholic Christians and Catholics is that the Protestant, on the whole, feels strongly that this is a private affair between himself and God; there is no room for a priest in it, no need for a sacrament.

Perhaps rejection of the sacrament on these lines would not have arisen but for the development of the sacrament itself in the direction of privacy. There is evidence that there *was* private confession and absolution even at a very early date in the Church; but the general aspect of sacramental absolution, in its early days, was that of a public reconciliation with the Church of those who were publicly known to have sinned away their right to live in her. It was a long liturgical process, spaced over months or even years; beginning with public penance outside the church door, and moving through various stages of partial admission to the Church's worship, until at last absolution was publicly given and the penitent received again into Communion. It was, in a sense, like a second baptism; it was regarded not so much as an ever-available remedy, but rather as a privileged second chance, after the first grace of baptismal forgiveness, which should really be the only one, had been forfeited.

To go on from this to as much as a third or a fourth chance seemed already a very doubtful possibility to the early Church. It was not, I think, that they had a *fundamentally* different notion of the possibility of forgiveness. Today, as then, the Church's minister must be convinced, in order to absolve, that the penitent is sincerely repentant. But nowadays there is a realization that countless falls *can* be followed by genuine repentance, even though another fall may follow again. It looks as though, for several centuries, Christians would have found it just conceivable that a man who had already contradicted his baptism once might really mean his second repentance, but practically incredible that one who then went on to contradict that second repentance too should, nevertheless, be sincere in yet a third conversion, let alone a fifth or a fiftieth. It is in her present hopeful readiness to recognize repentance as sincere, even after many falls, that the Church's approach has changed. Along with this goes a merciful leniency in the kind of "penance" imposed, a few short prayers to say, rather than long fastings or pilgrimage. And with this, too, goes the kindly emphasis on anonymous, confidential privacy.

All this is great gain to us. It makes the return of the prodigal easier, and it encourages us all, even the not-so-severely tempted, to use the power of sacramental absolution to help us in our daily struggle with venial sin, not only for bringing us to life again after mortal sin. But it would be good if we could have gain without loss. We may be in danger of losing sight of two truths that the earlier, stricter

4+

discipline emphasized: the horror of contradicting our baptism, and the essentially public nature of reconciliation with the Church.

However ready the Church mercifully is to give us absolution hundreds of times over, we ought to recognize that restoring divine life to us after mortal sin is not a routine, simply-to-be-counted-on affair. We should have it vividly in mind that it is, on the supernatural plane, something at the level of the raising of the dead on the natural plane. We should think of it in terms of Christ's three life-restoring miracles rather than of his countless healing miracles. To live the divine life in unbroken continuity from baptism to the grave ought to be normal Christianity. To slip into the completely opposite attitude, in which "a state of grace" is merely something you get into for special occasions, by going through the process of confession, and which does not much matter so long as you manage to be in it at the hour of death, would be a dreadful perversion of Christianity.

The second possible loss, forgetfulness of the essentially public nature of absolution, is, I have suggested, a possible root cause of the Protestant reaction against this sacrament. The general appearance of the sacrament of penance in the Church nowadays is that of a private affair; and if the forgiveness of our sins is a private affair, then the Protestant feeling that it is a private affair between ourselves and God rather than between ourselves and a priest seems reasonable and Christian.

We may stress, in answer, that the priest is there not in his own person but as God's representative; but why should God need a representative? We can only return, within this framework, as we do return, over and over again, to Christ's clear authorizing word, recorded by St. John. The answer to every individual objection is indeed there. "How can a mere man, a sinner, forgive sins?" But the Apostles were mere men, and sinners, and these words were said to them. "How can any forgiving power be needed but the redeeming power of Christ crucified?" But on the very evening of his resurrection day, here he is, clearly giving authority to men to administer to others the forgiveness which he himself has just won. This is entirely true and conclusive; yet it is not unreasonable for people to be not *wholly* satisfied with an explanation that Christ made it so, and therefore it is so. It is not arrogant or irreverent to feel unanswered until there is some understanding of *why* Christ should have made it so; he did not make things according to a certain pattern for no reason at all.

There are incidental helps given by the

sacrament of penance, in its present customary form, which may come to mind but which do not meet the difficulty. The confessional is an opportunity for advice and consolation, leading to advance in the Christian life. This is true, but the advice could quite well be given elsewhere, nor is it always given. It is not strictly what we go to confession for, though we may hope for such help. But if we are given bare absolution without one syllable of spiritual direction, we have still received the sacrament for which we came; the reason for the sacrament cannot lie in something extra, which is not part of it. Again, in the confessional we receive the *assurance* of forgiveness: but many Protestants have fully as much confidence that they are forgiven, without hearing any words of absolution, and not because of any mere feeling but because of their faith in God's word. Should we reduce the point of the sacrament to a comfort for the less trusting? There is a third help, which leads us in the right direction. By confession, we have to make acknowledgment of our sins, to face them as what they are—which can also be a help in seeing them in advance for what they are, in the deceptive time of temptation. We are putting ourselves on trial as responsible persons, submitting to a judgement as a recognition of reality. This is not a sufficient account of the sacrament if we leave it at the individual psychological level, but the idea of recognition of responsibility leads us back towards the public, social nature of the sacrament, which was so stressed in the early Church.

In fact, our sins and their forgiveness simply are not a private affair. This is not only because by every sin, even a venial sin of thought, we damage the common life of the body of Christ, and ought to recognize this in our repentance and seek reconciliation with our fellow-members. It is more radical: our whole relationship with God is not a private affair. Just as he did not create us as isolated individuals but as members of a race and of society, depending on our fellow-members, so he has redeemed us, in his own humanity, not as isolated individuals but as members of his body, the Church, and so members of one another. This truth is expressed through baptism; we receive our share in God's life not through some private, individual arrangement of our own but by this public, corporate act in which the community baptizes us, and we are baptized into membership of it. It does not seem surprising, then, that if we destroy this life in ourselves it should be restored not by a private, individual arrangement of our own but by a public, corporate act in which the community communicates life to us again by reconciling us with itself. Or rather, in all this, Christ baptizes us through an act of his body, the Church, into that body; Christ absolves us, again through an act of that body, reconciling us with it.

Once again, in this as in all things, God is not bound by his sacraments, though we are bound to use them. Suppose a person who has committed mortal sin turns from his sin towards God. He has destroyed the divine life in himself; he is incapable of any act of supernatural love. He can only, at most, recognize repentantly that he needs God, that without God he is utterly lost; and even to recognize this shows that he is already being helped by God.[1] What is going to transform this mere repentant recognition of his *need* for God's life into the actual possession of God's life, the state of grace? The appointed means is the sacrament of penance, just as the appointed means for the initial giving of this life is the sacrament of baptism. A merely fearful and hungry sorrow is enough to take us into the confessional, spiritually dead; the absolution makes us alive with divine life, so that we can

[1] This is all, by the nature of his case, that he *can* do. He cannot make an act of supernatural love, because in a state of mortal sin, he *has* no supernatural love. He can no more make an act of love than he can fly, however much he may have practised making acts of perfect contrition (which means, acts of supernatural love) from childhood.

love once more with divine love and be lovingly sorry for our sins: it is the very forgiveness of them which makes it possible for us to be properly sorry for them. But God can work this same transformation without the sacrament, or in anticipation of the sacrament. Someone, a non-Catholic, who knows nothing or at least honestly believes nothing about the sacrament of penance, can, when he turns to God in helpless repentance, be raised by him into the supernatural life. By its power he can then reach a truly loving sorrow, what we call an act of perfect contrition, which is at once the sign and the means of his forgiveness, and is a sheer grace from God. The same thing can happen to a Catholic; but in this case, he knows that the sacrament is the appointed means of forgiveness, and he would be simply rejecting the forgiveness he has already been given if he did not go on, as soon as possible, to seek sacramental reconciliation with the Church, through which all God's grace is given.

It is the social, public nature of absolution that makes sense of it, matching the social, public nature of baptism. Why should reconciliation be private, when initiation was public? However much, for reasons of kindly mercy, our being received as penitents be hedged round nowadays with confidential secrecy, we should recognize the priest in the confessional as representing the whole Church to us. He is not an individual intermediary between us and Christ; he is simply an organ of Christ in his body the Church; ears to hear, a mind to judge, a will and voice to absolve, used by Christ, who lives on in the world in the society which is his body and with which we must be reconciled if we wish to live in him. Again, like all the sacraments, penance brings us back to the Eucharist; for it is in sacramental Communion, in which Christ's physical body unites us together in his mystical body, that our reconciliation is finally sealed and perfected.

This social nature of penance comes out strongly in the Old Testament preparation for the sacrament, presupposed by Christ when he set about fashioning it for the life of his Church. Repentance and reconciliation with God was sought and expressed in the life of his people by the public acts of sin-offerings, and of the liturgy of the Day of Atonement. It is against that public and liturgical background that we must set such expressions of individual, personal contrition as the *Miserere*, the *De Profundis*, and the other "penitential psalms". Indeed, they are never really individualistic; there is always a sense of the whole people of God involved in them.

The clearest foreshadowing of the sacrament

in the Old Law stresses its communal nature
even more; for the clearest type of all is that of
national rather than individual repentance.
Israel's rescue through the Red Sea is the type
of baptism: that is the initiation of the holy
people of God. But just as the individual Christian may go back on his baptism by mortal sin,
so the people went back on their alliance with
God, over and over again, by falling into
idolatry and every kind of sin. And just as the
individual Christian can return to union with
God through penance, so the people were called
back to repentant renewal of the alliance by
the preaching of the Prophets. The theme runs
through all the Prophets, from Nathan, who
called King David to repentance, through Elias
onwards, and behind them it runs through the
Book of Judges; indeed, it is only a repetition
of the recurrent rebellions and returns of the
people which mark the story of Moses. We have
a most moving example of it in the Book of
Joel, which the Church reads to us at the beginning of Lent: "Now therefore saith the
Lord: Be converted to me with all your heart,
in fasting, and in weeping, and in mourning.
And rend your hearts, and not your garments,
and turn to the Lord your God: for he is
gracious and merciful, patient and rich in
mercy, and ready to repent of the evil." (Joel
2.12–13.) The whole prophecy should be read,

4*

especially as God's forgiveness culminates in that promise of the outpouring of the Spirit which was fulfilled on the day of Pentecost.

So this rich tradition of national, liturgical repentance and absolution was there already, as Christ's raw material for fashioning his sacrament. We can trace three lines in his fashioning of it. There is his teaching about God's ready forgiveness, for which he taught us to pray in the "Our Father", and which he represented in the parables of the Lost Sheep, the Lost Groat, and the Prodigal Son; not forgetting the warning parable of the servant who was forgiven, but who cancelled his own forgiveness by refusing to forgive his fellow-servant. There is his own personal absolution of individual sinners: the paralytic who was let down to him through the roof, the woman who anointed his feet, the woman taken in adultery, the repentant thief. And there was the promise to his Apostles that they were to hold authority in this matter: "Whatsoever you shall bind upon earth, shall be bound also in heaven: and whatsoever you shall loose upon earth, shall be loosed also in heaven" (Matt. 18.18); he is here preparing the sacrament itself, in which absolution will be given by apostolic authority.

All this is given its living power and reality by his death and resurrection. It was by that sacrifice that he obtained, for all men, the forgiveness that he had already given, in anticipation of it, to individual penitents. The same death and resurrection which effects forgiveness of sins in baptism effects it in absolution of sins after baptism; if we are to be raised from the dead by penance to the life into which we were first born by baptism, it can only be in union with the risen Christ. In him alone the indwelling Trinity can come to us or can return to us. So it is on the evening of Easter Sunday itself that he appears to the Apostles and gives them the authority to give and to restore the life of the Trinity to men. "Peace be to you", he said. "As the Father hath sent me, I also send you." Then, breathing on them (the sign of the Spirit, the breath of life): "Receive ye the Holy Ghost. Whose sins you shall forgive they are forgiven them, and whose sins you shall retain, they are retained." Thus the Son, through the Spirit, in the name of the Father, gives to his Apostles[1] the power to restore the life of the Trinity to men.

Christ's death, winning forgiveness, and his resurrection, restoring life, are in action in this

[1] That the men addressed were, strictly, the Apostles, is plain from the special *sending* of them made here. When Christ named the Twelve his "apostles" (Luke 6.13), he was calling them "Those whom I am specially sending", since "apostle" means "sent". The power to forgive and to retain is here given to those who are thus specially sent.

rite of absolution which he gave. Anyone who has recourse to it is, by his power, formally reconciled with the community of the Church, and, provided that he has sought that reconciliation sincerely, is thus raised to life again as a member of the body of Christ, able once again to join with the rest of the Church in offering Christ's sacrifice and feeding upon his eucharistic body. It looks back in the past to the death on the Cross, through which alone all sin is forgiven; it acts here in the present, healing the wounds of the body of Christ; and it looks to that future when the lord of the household, the shepherd of the whole flock, will return. It is his desire that not one member shall be lost: the sheep that strays, the groat of the Church's treasure of souls that falls into darkness, must be found and recovered. Punishment for sin is meant to be for healing, a prelude to absolution. St. Paul, in sentencing the incestuous Corinthian to excommunication, says that it is so "that the spirit may be saved in the day of our Lord Jesus Christ". (1 Cor. 5.5.) In that day, the fullness of the body of Christ is to be complete; penance is the means mercifully provided by which no member need be lost, even though temporarily fallen away.

4. ANOINTING OF THE SICK

"Extreme unction", the more usual English name for this sacrament, if it can be called English, could hardly be more unfortunate. "Unction," nowadays, suggests an unpleasing manner of speech and behaviour, at once oily and gushing, while "extreme" simply underlines and intensifies it; and even this involves more understanding of the words than that possessed by one heckler at a Catholic Evidence Guild meeting, for whom extreme unction was a particularly cruel torture inflicted in convents, so severe that the poor nun almost always died after it.

To give the two words their equivalent in ordinary English would produce "last anointing", which is far preferable. But even this is apt to be misleading, though it need not be. It is taken as meaning "the anointing which we have in our last hours", thus labelling it as the sacrament of the dying: precisely the basic misunderstanding of it. What it actually means is "last of the anointings": if we make a list of the anointings which the Church uses, this will be the last in the list. There are the anointings associated with baptism, the anointing of confirmation, the anointing of the priest's hands during the ceremony of holy orders; and there is the anointing of the sick. If we could get into the habit of calling it the anointing of the sick, we should cease to mislead ourselves and others.

This is not, essentially, the sacrament of preparation for death. A Christian is prepared for death by being in a state of grace; any Catholic who knows he is in, or going into, danger of death, will naturally, if possible, confess and be absolved, even if he trusts he is already, as he should be, in a state of grace. The final sacramental preparation for death is the sacrament which is the climax and centre of all the seven, the Eucharist. When the Church gives us our last Communion, she calls it "Viaticum", company for our journey from this life to the next. (Of course, prediction is uncertain, and we may survive; if so, then it was not, after all, Viaticum, which is simply a name for our last Communion before death.) We have in it a last sacramental meeting with Christ before meeting him face to face. These are the sacraments of the dying: Viaticum, fittingly preceded by sacramental absolution. They could, and should, be received by those going into battle or any deadly danger, those facing execution, and those in the last stages of a killing disease or fatal injury. But it is only the last of these three classes who could be given the anointing; for it is not an anointing for death, in which case it could be given to all these, but an anointing of the sick. It is concerned with sickness, not with the end of life; it is concerned not *primarily* with preparation for death, but with healing.

This does not mean that it is unconnected with preparation for death, as we shall see. But we can take St. James' description of it at its face value. When he says of a sick man whom the priests have anointed in the name of the Lord that "the prayer of faith shall save the sick man, and the Lord shall raise him up" (James 5.15), we do not have to "spiritualize" it into some allegorical meaning; St. James is telling us that we should expect the patient to recover.

To some, a sacrament for healing seems a strange and contradictory thing; disease and health are strictly a matter of this natural life, while the sacraments give us supernatural life. But this brings us back to that final, uncompromising Christian assertion of the body-soul unity of man: "I believe in the resurrection of the body." The body itself is to be involved in the supernatural order: indeed, it already is so in Christ's body, in which we are redeemed. Hence we ought not to be surprised to find a sacrament so deeply concerned with the body. Moreover, disease is not just a sort of accident. Man's illnesses are an evil, an upsetting of the right pattern of things, which ought not to have happened. They are a result of the Fall. Unfallen man would not have been ill; by a special gift, his spirit would always have shaped and dominated the matter of his body so completely that it would neither have suffered damage from outside nor worn out by use. Disease is part of the reign of the devil in this world, a reign begun when man first surrendered to the devil. Christ's redemption of the world was a defeat of the devil: "Now shall the prince of this world be cast out", he said. (John 12.31.)

But we do die. Even though we may have been anointed, for our healing, in several illnesses, the time normally comes when we have a last illness, and do not recover after anointing, but die. Does this mean that Christ was not after all victorious, that the sacrament is ineffectual? No: for the final redeeming, the total healing of our bodies can only come in their final resurrection at the Last Day. All healings in this life, which are always only partial, are foreshadowings of that. It would be equally wrong to despise them (which would mean despising a large part of Christ's public ministry) and to regard them as the final good. Because disease is wrong and health is right, God heals us of our diseases in this life by every kind of means, medicine and miracles included. He has given us a sacrament of healing, which is not intended, at least generally, to work by miracle, but through the ordinary power of the spirit to enliven the body; hence it should not be given in the last stages when hope of recovery is practically gone, but whenever there is illness of a serious, dangerous nature. What we look for from this sacrament is healing.

But a time comes for each of us when God, who knows us utterly, sees that there can be no further healing for us but the full and final healing of the Resurrection; and the body's last stage before that, the anaesthetic before the operation, so to speak, is death. If anointing is followed by death rather than recovery, it is not because the sacrament is not, after all, or not in this case, a healing sacrament, but because the time has come for a total healing. How does the sacrament serve this total healing?

St. Thomas Aquinas tells us that it remedies the weariness of spirit which may prevent the last illness from being a good spiritual preparation for death; and that it takes away the "remains" of sin, making purgatory, it is to be hoped, unnecessary. St. James, indeed, concludes his description of the effects of the sacrament with "and if he be in sins, they shall be forgiven him". The Church does not regard anointing of the sick as a substitute for the sacrament of penance, except for a patient who has lost consciousness, when anointing can indeed remit mortal sins, repented, perhaps imperfectly, and not absolved. But otherwise it is a "sacrament of the living", like all the rest except baptism and penance, meaning that it is to be received in a state of grace. The being "in sins" of which St. James speaks here is, in general, the imperfect state in which our repentance usually still leaves us; our sorrow is seldom so radical, so completely generous, that it allows God to refashion us in one stroke into the image of himself which we are meant to be. Hence he continues this refashioning of us, this gradual complete "conversion" of us, through all the experiences, prayers, good works and sufferings of our lives. It is because this refashioning may still be incomplete (because of our hindrance of it) at the time of death, that we may need purgatory. But, St. Thomas says, the sacrament of anointing is meant to complete the purifying of us, healing the remaining scars of our sins, so that we should not need purgatory: it is an "anointing for glory". We can easily see this as part of the healing which is to be completed in the Resurrection.

In this last of the anointings, then, a sick Christian is consecrated, in his sickness, to God; this dedication of the patient is the *res et sacra-*

mentum, the sign-reality of this sacrament, infallibly accomplished by its administration. If it is received with proper dispositions, it then effects its *res tantum,* the sheer reality of its proper spiritual effect. This means the sanctification of the person in and through his illness, so that the illness, as an experience, becomes all that God wills it to be: a deepening of the Christian life, with the healing power of the sacrament strengthening the spirit against the effects of bodily suffering, removing the scars of sin, and so preparing either for the healing of ordinary recovery and a return to the active life of the Church on earth, or for the total healing of death and resurrection. Again, we must remember how all the sacraments face towards the Eucharist; the Blessed Sacrament will normally be received after anointing of the sick, either as Viaticum or as a strengthening of soul and body. And if the anointing leads to normal recovery, then the high point of that recovery will be the return to an active share in the sacrificial, eucharistic life of the Church.

As the sacrament of healing, anointing of the sick has its roots in all the natural activity of man's fight against disease in medicine and nursing, from the most primitive attempts at remedies, whether helpful or disastrous, to the latest developments in medicine and surgery.

The command of our Lord to go and heal the sick is not only carried out by miracle-workers, but by all those engaged in the service of the sick.

When we turn to the Old Testament, we find the sacrament of healing foreshadowed by God's interventions in regard to illness. There is the tremendously significant incident of the brazen serpent in Num. 21.6–9. Its significance lies in Christ's application of it to himself: "As Moses lifted up the serpent in the desert, so must the Son of man be lifted up." (John 3.14.) This means that the brazen serpent is a type of Christ crucified, the Redeemer; as those who looked upon the brazen serpent were healed of snake-bite, so those who look to Christ are saved from the devil. As a type of the whole Redemption, it certainly cannot be narrowed down to one sacrament; but there is no reason why we should not see it in its application to one aspect of Christ's saving work. The Israelites, bitten by the poisonous serpents, were healed through an outward sign, and that a sign of Christ on the Cross; we are healed of sickness by an outward sign which, like all the sacraments, is a sign of Christ in his death and resurrection.

There are further healing interventions of God's power when we come to the miracles of

Elias and Eliseus. The cure of Naaman the Leper by bathing in the Jordan (4 Kings 5) is a type of baptism; but it is also a healing of disease, and so a foreshadowing of anointing of the sick. And there is the touching story of King Ezechias who, when he fell sick, was told by Isaias that he was about to die, but would not take this as God's last word, and wept and prayed for life, so that the Lord granted him fifteen years more. (4 Kings 20.) The story emphasizes the theme that recovery from illness means a return to the liturgical worship of God: "I have heard thy prayer and I have seen thy tears," is God's second message through Isaias, "and behold I have healed thee; on the third day thou shalt go up to the temple of the Lord."

The climax of the theme of healing in the Old Testament comes in one of those prophetical promises of national restoration which we can see as looking beyond the immediate situation to the coming of Christ's kingdom of grace. It is the thirty-fifth chapter of Isaias: "God himself will come and save you. Then shall the eyes of the blind be opened, and the ears of the deaf shall be unstopped. Then shall the lame man leap as a hart, and the tongue of the dumb shall be free: for waters are broken out in the desert, and streams in the wilderness." Before our Lord's time this was already understood as a prophecy of what would be happening in the messianic age, when God's kingdom would come upon earth. So our Lord himself refers to it when the disciples of John the Baptist are sent to ask him, "Art thou he who is to come?" Christ's answer is, "Go and relate to John what you have heard and seen: the blind see, the lame walk, the lepers are made clean, the deaf hear, the dead rise again, to the poor the Gospel is preached." (Luke 7.20–2.)

And so we are brought to Christ's own making of the sacrament of anointing the sick. It is rather like the making of the sacrament of penance. There we have Christ's own individual pardonings, his delegation to the Apostles of the power to absolve, and, giving life to all this, his pardon-obtaining death and resurrection. Here, we have all of his healing miracles, his command to the Apostles to heal, and his filling of their healing ministry with the dynamic effect of his own painful death and life-giving resurrection.

First, his healing miracles. It is shocking if we allow ourselves to regard them as mere demonstrations of power, done simply to prove his divine authority, as though Christ would say to a leper, "Yes, I will make you clean, not because I care for you but in order to prove that I am God." Only once did he say anything faintly resembling this, when he showed that his healing of the paralytic established his right to forgive sins. (Matt. 9.6.) He did indeed sometimes point to his miracles as a sort of last resort: If you cannot believe in me, at least believe them. (John 10.25, 38: 14.12: 15.24.) But this is a second best; he rebukes those who look for signs and wonders. (John 4.48; Matt. 16.4.) When he refers John's disciples to his miracles, it is not as a mere demonstration of power. Miracles are signs of the messianic age first and foremost because healing is good rather than because it is wonderful. The coming of healing means the coming of life, of God's reign upon earth.

For disease is part of the devil's reign. Our Lord makes this clear in his healing of the deformed woman in Luke 13: "And ought not this daughter of Abraham, whom Satan hath bound, lo, these eighteen years, be loosed from this bond on the sabbath day?" His endless merciful acts of healing were a part of his battle with Satan, like his casting out of devils and his forgiveness of sins. The opening of the battle was the temptation in the desert, the triumphant climax was the death and resurrection. And this whole battle was fought out by our Lord in his *human* nature. He could only do it because he was personally God: but he did it all, the whole victorious battle of our redemption, *as man*. So, though there are healing miracles which stress the divine sovereignty of the person who is doing them—those done at a distance, for instance, or the "I will: be thou made clean" cure of a leper—yet there are many indications elsewhere that Christ's work of healing really was work. He could feel strength going out from him when he healed (Mark 5.30); the stories of the healing of the deaf and dumb man (Mark 7.32–7) and of the blind man in the next chapter give a picture of Christ as it were wrestling with the evil of deafness and blindness, as he said that it was necessary to wrestle, by prayer and fasting, with the devil of epilepsy in the following chapter. (Mark 9.)

His work of healing was a part of the heavily costing battle with the devil which he completed in triumph on the Cross. It was on the Cross that he won, through the sufferings and death of his own body, the grace which heals the bodies of others; the final, perfect healing of them is the reproducing in them of the resurrection first accomplished in him. St. Matthew gives us the key to this by applying to Christ's healing of the sick the great prophecy of the Passion in Isaias, Chapter 53. "And all that were sick he healed: that it might be fulfilled, which was spoken by the prophet Isaias, saying: He took our infirmities, and bore our diseases." (Matt. 8.16–17.) He did not only heal them, he *bore* them: in the exacting work of his ministry and in the sufferings and death which ended it. By his own bearing of them he provided healing for them, both in the recoveries which are an image of the Resurrection in this life and in the perfect healing of the final Resurrection.

At the same time, he provided the sacramental sign by which healing was to be given in the Church. When he sent out his twelve apostles to preach during his own lifetime, he gave them power "to heal all manner of diseases, and all manner of infirmities" (Matt. 10.1), and he repeated the command to heal the sick to the seventy-two disciples whose mission is described in Luke 10. This power the Church, of which the Apostles were the beginning, has to this day; not to make miraculous cures of any and every case of illness, but to bring sacramental healing to "all manner", to every kind, of disease and infirmity. Healing *miracles* still follow, from time to time, the course of the Church's life, as he promised they would (Mark 16.17–18); but the general power to heal granted to the Apostles is wider than that. In St. Mark's gospel (6.13) we read that even on their first mission the Apostles used anointing with oil in their healing of the sick. This would not yet be the sacrament, for the same reason that their baptizing at that time was not yet Christian baptism (because Jesus was not yet sacrificed and glorified). But it is already the sign of the sacrament, ready for Christ to fill it with sacramental power by his death and resurrection.

The healing power of his sufferings, his death, his resurrection is, then, present in this rite which he gave to the Church. By it the sick are dedicated to God in their sickness, so that, by the grace which it gives, their sickness may become whatever God wills: an occasion for temporary healing or a preparation for the final healing in which the redemption of our bodies will be completed in the glorious Resurrection.

5. MARRIAGE

Marriage (in the sense of sexual union) is as basic and ancient a religious symbol as even water is.[1] The union of man with woman gives an image of the longed-for union of God with humanity, and fertility is a symbol of the gift of divine life. This image in the mind of man was given its full realization in the union of God with man accomplished in the marriage of Christ with his bride, the Church. It is in

[1] See Eliade, *Patterns in Comparative Religion*, especially chapters 2, "The Sky and Sky Gods", 7, "The Earth, Woman, and Fertility" and 9, "Agricultural and Fertility Cults".

virtue of that transcendant marriage, in which Christ himself is the bridegroom, that Christian marriage is a sacrament.

The word "marriage" can be used, purely descriptively, to mean all types of union between men and women, however various, which have been recognized and sanctioned by society rather than merely practised by individuals. In this sense a study of "marriage" would include polygamy, polyandry, divorce, marriage by capture, etc. But the word can also be used dogmatically to mean the one form of such union which is or ever has been intended and fully approved by God; a lifelong union between one man and one woman, excluding all others, entered into by the free consent of both parties. Departures from this pattern, even though a part of the history of God's chosen people, were always a departure from the true created pattern of marriage, and were merely tolerated and not approved by God. We can be certain of this from the comment of our Lord upon the Mosaic law of divorce: such licence was given because of "hardness of heart", not because it corresponded to the true nature of marriage: "From the beginning it was not so", but marriage was, as created, a union of "two in one flesh". (Matt. 19.6, 8.)

Even where it is not a sacrament, marriage already involves a special intervention of God.

For though the initial and obvious element in it is the marriage contract made by the man and woman, their marriage does not simply consist of that contract. Whenever the contract is validly made, God responds to the making of it by creating between the parties the husband-wife relationship. This relationship is as real and permanent as the relationships of parent-child or brother-sister, etc., which God creates in response to the human act of generation. It is the marriage relationship, created by God between the parties in response to their free contract, which unites them together for life. Since the relationship is made by God, it could be dissolved only by God, as we have it in our Lord's words: "What God hath joined together, let no man put asunder." (Matt. 19.6.)

It is this reality of marriage, the human contract sealed by the divinely created relationship, which Christ has made into a sacrament of the New Law. In order to look properly at his making of it, we must begin again with the preparation of his material in the Old Testament.

We begin with the creation of man and woman. "And God created man to his own image: to the image of God he created him: male and female he created them." (Gen. 1.27.) In this first creation story, there seems even a hint that being male and female is included in being in the image of God. Not that God is male and female (nor male); but, looking back through the later revelation of the Trinity, we can see the giving and receiving between the sexes as an image of the giving and receiving in God himself.

In the second picture of creation, in Chapter 2 of Genesis, we have a vivid instruction on the nature of marriage. When Adam found himself without any equal companion in all creation, God took man's own bone and flesh and made a woman of it. We could not find a clearer statement that man and woman are of one substance, in essential equality, and Adam hails his wife as "bone of my bones, and flesh of my flesh". The final comment is, "Wherefore a man shall leave father and mother, and shall cleave to his wife: and they shall be two in one flesh"—the essential pattern of marriage to which Christ's teaching returned.

Such is the gift of marriage in which the Church rejoices during the Nuptial Mass; a blessing which was neither lost by the Fall nor destroyed in the Flood. But though it was not lost by the Fall, it was certainly damaged. Part of God's reproach to Adam in Chapter 3 is, "Because thou hast hearkened to the voice of thy wife . . ."; and the sentence of Eve includes, "Thou shalt be under thy husband's power, and he shall have dominion over thee." Woman the temptress calls into being man the tyrant. The war of the sexes is on, and is one of the deep wounds in human nature. The healing is far away, in Christ's redemptive act, expressed in the sacrament of marriage.

Because God was going to bring redemption by being himself born into the human race, with a long preparation of human ancestry, the succession of generations, of marriages and births, is an important part of the preparation for his coming. Particular individual marriages prepare the way for the coming of the Redeemer, and so for the healing of marriage itself. The birth of Isaac, by God's promise, to the seemingly-barren Sarah; the search for a bride for Isaac from among his own people; the choice of Jacob over Esau, even in Rebecca's womb; the love of Jacob for Rachel, his unwilling marriage with her sister Lia, who became the mother of Juda and so the ancestress of Jesus—all these events are part of the building up of history towards Christ, in which marriage, damaged and as yet unhealed, has to play its part and so already receives a certain sanctification to be completed by Christ himself. Hence the Church recalls the names of the wives of the Patriarchs—Sarah the old and faithful, Rebecca the wise (if not very attractively so), Rachel the beloved—during the blessing of the bride in the Nuptial Mass.

Surely the most moving story of all those we are told of the marriages which prepared for Christ is that in the Book of Ruth. Its loveliness appeals to us still, however surprised we may be by such power in a story whose mainspring is the seemingly-remote notion of the Levirate marriage: the duty of a man's kinsman, if the man himself died without an heir, to marry his widow and give a legal heir to a branch of the family which would otherwise die out. In the mouths of the Sadducees of our Lord's time, this law was an occasion for the stupidest type of superficial heckling about the final resurrection. Under the hand of the inspired writer of the Book of Ruth, it is the basis of a story which, in its own right, can move and delight us still, and can be truly called a love-story, though the love it portrays is not that of man and woman but of a daughter-in-law for her mother-in-law. Its place in the Bible, however, is due less to its intrinsic beauty than to its record of the ancestry of David; and this too is its importance in Christian eyes: "And Booz begot Obed, of Ruth" (Matt. 1.5)—part of the genealogy of Christ. This book well emphasizes the dominating note in Old Testament thought on marriage; a longing, one might say a grimly determined longing, for offspring. And this is not only the natural, universal desire for fruitfulness but the persistent sense of a vocation to build up through the centuries the People of God, whether or not consciously connected with the birth of a future Messiah.

Along with this sanctification, in terms of the vocation of the People of God, of concrete, individual human marriages, there is another Old Testament marriage theme which is preparing for Christ; for the redemption as a whole, and for the redemption of marriage within that whole. This is the theme of the marriage of God with his people. It appears in the prophecy of Osee, amidst reproaches for the infidelity of the bride but with an indestructible tenderness: "And I will espouse thee to me for ever: and I will espouse thee to me in justice, and judgement, and in mercy, and in commiserations. And I will espouse thee to me in faith: and thou shalt know that I am the Lord." (Osee 2.19–20.) Jeremias takes up the theme (chapters 2 and 3), Ezechiel develops it in his sixteenth and twenty-third chapters: "And I passed by thee and saw thee: and behold thy time was the time of lovers: and I spread my garment over thee and covered thy ignominy. And I swore to thee, and I entered into a covenant with thee, saith the Lord God: and thou becamest mine." (Ezech. 16.8.) The later part of the Book of Isaias, proclaiming the restoration of Israel to God's

favour, uses the same image again. And in the
Song of Songs, the allegory is developed with
such lavishness and intensity that interpreters
dispute among themselves whether its primary
meaning is concerned with human or divine
love. For how could such uninhibited sen-
suality be an account of God's spiritual marriage with his people? And how, on the other
hand, could such exuberance, if found in Holy
Writ at all, be justified by any lesser theme? It
is more commonly held that we do indeed have
here the expression of God's marriage, and
reacceptance, after the seeming divorce of the
captivity, of his people; but the manner of its
treatment makes it also the expression of God's
delight in human marriage.

When our Lord came, then, there were already these three themes in readiness for him:
that marriage is, in its original, created fresh-
ness, the exclusive, permanent relationship of
two in one flesh; that it is part not only of
the general vocation of mankind but of the
special vocation of God's people, building up,
generation by generation, towards the fulfilment of God's purpose in history; and that it
is an image of God's self-giving union with his
people. Christ now shows himself as the fulfilment of that union, the true Bridegroom; and
he makes of each particular Christian marriage
not merely an image but a sacramental repre-

sentation of that union, so filled with the redeeming grace of his death and resurrection that it is itself a means of grace like the other sacraments, and has its special significance in the building up of the body of Christ, generation by generation, towards its fulfilment in his second coming.

Christ's work upon marriage begins with his coming into the world as the child of Mary, Joseph's wife, and his hallowing of family life by living it himself. But a difficulty occurs to us here. Does not his virgin birth, whatever other significance it has, represent, in this sphere at least, a certain refusal on his part to take hold on human marriage in its fullness? This is not the place, nor the writer, for a consideration of the full meaning of the Virgin Birth in its relation to the incarnation of God the Son (for which it was not strictly necessary, but which it does show forth in a special way), or its place in God's whole scheme of redemption, including his mother's role in it. But we do need to reach some notion of its connection with the redemption of marriage. Perhaps we can see that there can be no sanctification without renunciation: the Holy Family, which was the beginning of the final sanctification of marriage, was itself founded upon a marriage in which renunciation, even of the natural marital privileges, was total. It is the mystery of the seed which must die in order to bear fruit; no ordinary marriage could have been such a total new beginning.

"And the third day, there was a marriage in Cana of Galilee: and the mother of Jesus was there. And Jesus also was invited, and his disciples, to the marriage." Some of the Church's commentators have seen our Lord's presence at this marriage, and his working of his first miracle there, as itself the definite institution of the sacrament. Whether this is so or not, it is certainly a part of his making of it. The very name of the village is significant. It reminds us of Canaan, the old name of the Holy Land when it was not a holy land but a land of nature-worshipping paganism. The name could well stand for all fertile, sensual, natural life, as yet unredeemed. Here Christ sanctifies marriage by his presence and his miracle; a miracle worked at his mother's request, a miracle of the Holy Family. And the actual miracle proclaims what redemption means to nature itself: not a weakening and diluting, not wine into water, but strengthening and enriching, water into wine.

His beginning of his miracles at a marriage already gives a hint of Christ as the true Bridegroom, and in the next chapter of St. John's gospel we have John the Baptist applying this title to him. (John 3.29.) He himself appeals to it when reproached because his disciples do not lead an ascetic life: "Can the children of the marriage fast, as long as the bridegroom is with them? As long as the bridegroom is with them, they cannot fast." (Mark 2.19.) In its implication that he is the fulfilment of the marriage of God with Israel, it is a declaration of his divinity; and he develops it in his parable of the wedding-feast: "The kingdom of heaven is likened to a king who made a marriage for his son." (Matt. 22.2.) The time has come: God, the king, is making a marriage for his Son, who is truly God. The bridegroom is here, all things are ready, come to the marriage. But the invited guests, the chosen people, are turning their backs and will not come. Yet the marriage must still take place; indeed, it is their very rejection which will lead to its consummation, on the Cross.

The paradox is that while the marriage has taken place, yet we are still looking forward to it. It is in the vision of the Apocalypse that we are told to "be glad and rejoice, and give glory to God: for the marriage of the Lamb is come, and his wife hath prepared herself" (Apoc. 19.7); and though this is a vision of the life of the Church here and now, it is also a vision of the Last Things. We are at present in the time of waiting: "The time will come when the bridegroom will be taken

away from them, and then they will fast."
(Mark 2.20.) We are all of us standing (or
sleeping) in wait, hoping that our lamps will
be burning clear when the cry is made, "Behold the bridegroom cometh, go ye forth to
meet him." (Matt. 25.6.) And it is to this
interim period that Christian marriage, the
sacramental representation of Christ's marriage, belongs, as do all the sacraments.

Before his final act of death and resurrection
which fills it with grace, Christ has restored
marriage to its original perfection. This restoration, like his act at Cana, has been regarded as
the actual institution of the sacrament. We do
not know whether he may have made some
other, unrecorded, even more explicit institution. But this teaching, recorded at the beginning of St. Matthew's nineteenth chapter, does
seem almost explicitly to place marriage in the
sacramental order by being, so deliberately, an
act of the New Creation. "From the beginning
it was not so" are the words that sweep away
all intervening distortions of the pattern, divorce or polygamy. "He who made man from
the beginning made them male and female. For
this cause shall a man leave father and mother
and shall cleave to his wife, and they two shall
be in one flesh. Therefore now they are not
two, but one flesh. What therefore God hath
joined together, let no man put asunder."

Here is the sign, restored in the Redeemer's new creation to what it was in the first creation. Then, in his final sacrifice, the New Adam filled it with the power to be, as a sacrament, a living and effective sign of his own marriage, in which the Church, his bride, came forth from his side as he slept upon the Cross. It is in terms of that marriage, in which we, as members of the Church, are united with Christ the Head, that St. Paul sees Christian marriage. "The husband is the head of the wife, as Christ is the head of the church . . . Therefore as the church is subject to Christ, so also let the wives be to their husbands in all things. Husbands, love your wives, as Christ also loved the church, and delivered himself up for it . . . So also ought men to love their wives as their own bodies. He that loveth his wife, loveth himself. For no man ever hated his own flesh; but nourisheth and cherisheth it, as also Christ doth the church: because we are members of his body, of his flesh and of his bones. 'For this cause shall a man leave his father and mother, and shall cleave to his wife, and they shall be two in one flesh.' This is a great sacrament; but I speak in Christ and in the church." (Eph. 5.23–32.)

St. Paul sees that in Christian marriage the relationship of two-in-one-flesh is no longer grounded simply in human nature but rather in our membership of Christ; it is their union with Christ that unites husband and wife, and this is another way of saying that their marriage is a sacrament. (But we should not interpret the Douai translation of St. Paul's last sentence here as an early use of the word "sacrament" in its later, developed, specialized sense: he is saying that the union of Christ and the Church is a great mystery, of which the word "sacrament" is the Latin equivalent.)

Thus the power of Christ's redemptive sacrifice, in its aspect as a marriage, is in each Christian union, making it a sacramental union with himself. It is because it is a sacrament that it is under the Church's jurisdiction, just as its importance in natural social life brings it legitimately under the supervision of the State. The Church, in her governance of it as a sacrament, can and does make conditions for its valid performance; at the present day she requires that for a Catholic to make a valid marriage the contract must be witnessed by a duly authorized priest. For non-Catholics, she makes no such condition, naturally. Wherever two baptized persons, whether Catholics or not, make a valid marriage contract, they confer upon each other, as ministers of the sacrament, this source of grace in which they become a living image of the union of Christ with his church. The unbreakable relationship which thus exists between them is the unfailing effect, the *res et sacramentum*, the sign-reality, of this sacrament. So long as the couple are in a state of grace at the time of conferring it, it will give its own sacramental grace, the *res tantum*, the sheer reality, which is the proper result of the sacrament. This is the grace to become married saints, building up the body of Christ towards its final completion, through the life of a Christian family, in which husband and wife co-operate, by human, bodily lovemaking, with God's creation of new human beings.

This means, of course, that the grace of the sacrament of marriage is a permanent grace, lasting down the years like that of baptism, confirmation and orders, even though it does not, as they do, effect that unique, unrepeatable change in a person, in his relationship to Christ in his priesthood, which is called the seal. But, like them, it is something that remains; as sacramentally present, as actively effective, years afterwards as on the wedding day. It is one consequence of this that, if the grace of the sacrament was refused that first day by the sacrilege of contracting marriage in mortal sin, it can yet be fully received later on, by repentance; for the relationship which is the sign-reality is there, permanently, ready to be brought to supernatural life.

This applies, too, to a non-sacramental marriage, validly contracted between people who are not baptized. They have already made the sign: and if they are later baptized, the supernatural reality is at once added to the sign, without further ceremony, so that their marriage is at once a sacrament.[1]

This is a sacrament whose end is in a special way the welfare of the community, the body of Christ. Marriages and families are building up that body towards its full stature. Such building-up can only be done by the power of the sacrament of unity, the Eucharist. A Christian family community is essentially a preparation and training for the eucharistic community; hence a Catholic marriage is fittingly celebrated with full participation, by Communion, in the Nuptial Mass.

The final goal of this building up of the body is the second coming of the Bridegroom and the resurrection of those whose lives have served the completion of his body, the Church, which is his bride. Then there will be no more marriage; for the image will no longer be needed when the marriage of the Lamb has come and the full number of the human

[1] It has sometimes been held that in a marriage between a baptized and a non-baptized person, the baptized person does receive the sacrament, which must be administered to him, in that case (as baptism itself can be) by an unbaptized minister.

5*

race is complete. But he will surely bring the
fulfilment, not the destruction, of the loving
friendship to which the grace of marriage leads;
and surely, too, the bodies which rise again will
have a special glory from that right use of their
bodily powers which they made in the sacrament of marriage.

6. ORDERS

Orders is the third of the "sealing" sacraments, which means that it is the one which
most completely of all identifies a man with
Christ in his priesthood. Christ is the one
priest: that is, the one man who gives to God
perfect worship on behalf of the whole human
race. To worship is to give the honour that is
due, what the person, or thing, is *worth*; and
towards God that is something which we, as
human beings, cannot do. To begin with, it is
not possible for even the most perfect of crea-
tures, being limited in all it does, to give to
the infinite Creator honour which would truly
express what he in himself is worth. But there
is another sense of giving what is due: giving
all of which the creature, in accordance with
God's pattern for it, is capable, and so giving
what is due as from it. Now, by the ruin of
the Fall, man became incapable of rendering
what is due to God even in this relative sense.

But when Christ brings redemption, it is more than mere restoration. Not only does he restore mankind to the supernatural relationship in which man can render to God homage as worthy of him (relatively speaking) as it could have been before the Fall. He made the redemption by offering perfect worship himself, as man. The person who was God the Son gave perfect honour to the Father, such as only the infinite divine person could give: and he gave it in his own human nature, so that it was truly human worship, but with that fullness of the meaning of "worship" which no act of a human person could have been, even without the Fall.

Christ is the Priest, giving, in his own person and in his human nature, perfect worship to God. We share in his worship, in his priesthood, by being made one with him. Baptism already makes us one with him in a priestly sense: we are members of his body, in which his worship of God is continued upon earth. Confirmation is a further initiation into his priesthood in making us spiritually mature members of the worshipping body, with an official commission to perform that part of its worship which consists in witnessing to God's truth in this world. Those who are ordained are identified with Christ the Priest in a still deeper sense; this sacrament makes men, already members of Christ's body, into organs within it which are immediate instruments of the continuation of Christ's worship.

We may distinguish three aspects of Christ's worship, and so of the worship of his body, the Church. First, it was a perfect human worship of God that there should simply exist one man totally pleasing to God, full of grace, good in all that he was and did. This aspect of his worship is continued by the sheer existence of the Church as the community which is God's kingdom, God's household in this world; united in grace, in obedience, in good works. Secondly, Christ gave honour to God by witnessing to divine truth in this world, by his teaching. The Church's faith is worship, honouring God by bearing witness down the ages, by the power of the Spirit, to revealed truth. Thirdly, Christ summed up the worship of his whole life in the sacrifice of his death on Calvary, where he was both priest and victim, giving to the Father the most complete worship possible in his human nature through the total self-giving of a painful death. The Church offers this same sacrifice, in which now there is no suffering or death, under the sacramental signs of bread and wine which he himself gave the night before he suffered.

It is easy to associate the three sacraments of initiation into Christ's priesthood with these

three aspects of his worship. Baptism makes us
members of that body which honours God
simply by existing as the redeemed community
of grace; confirmation is the sacrament of witness; and orders gives a man the power to
make Christ's sacrifice present under the signs
of bread and wine. This is true, but it is equally
true that all three sacraments are related to all
three aspects of Christ's worship, for they are
not divided but all one. Baptism makes us
members of the community which *is* the
witnessing and sacrificing community. Confirmation makes us, personally and responsibly,
witnesses; and this confirms and deepens our
relationship to the whole life of the community
and its sacrifice in particular. And the man
who is ordained has a new and special relationship to every aspect of the Church's life, not
just to the ritual sacrifice.

The life of the community, simply as a community, is built upon obedience. The authority
involved is meant to be exercised only in the
extreme of humility: "Whosoever will be first
among you, shall be the servant of all." (Mark
10.44.) But it is real authority: the body of
Christ is a kingdom in which men hold office
as judges (Luke 22.29–30), a household in
which men hold office as stewards. (Matt.
24.45–51; 1 Cor. 4.1.) Ordination includes a
man among the stewards and judges, dispens-

ing grace through the sacraments and making authoritative decisions; and this lays on him, too, the obligation to be an example to the rest of the community in its life of good works.

The same hierarchy who are in charge of the general life of the community, as a household, are also in charge of its worship of witnessing to God's truth in the world. It is they who hold from Christ the commission to teach, with the guarantee of his own presence and the guidance of the Holy Spirit to preserve their teaching from corruption. Through the exercise of their teaching office, the witness of the community is preserved as a witness to God's truth, prevented from turning into a spreading of human error.

Thirdly, besides being ordained as ruler and teacher in God's household, the priest is a sacrificing priest. It is by his ministry that the sacrifice of Christ is made sacramentally present so that the whole body of Christ can share in the crown and consummation of his worship.

So, in the New Israel, the Church of Christ, there is a relationship between the community as a whole and a special ministry within it which corresponds to a similar relationship in the Old Israel, the Church of the Old Testament. In both, the whole people is a priestly community. "Thou has made us to our God a kingdom and priests", say the redeemed in the Apocalypse (5.10); and St. Peter says to all the baptized, "You are a chosen generation, a kingly priesthood, a holy nation, a purchased people." (1 Pet. 2.9.) Both are echoing the Book of Exodus, where God tells his people at the time of his covenant with them that they are henceforth a nation of priests. (Exod. 19.6.) Just as in the Old Israel there was, within the whole priestly nation, an order of priests, Aaron and his descendants, who offered the sacrifices of the people, so in the New Israel, the body of Christ, there is an order of priests who, under sacramental signs, offer the one sacrifice in which the whole people joins.

The priesthood of Aaron is one Old Testament preparation for the New Testament priesthood, but a limited one. The task of exercising general authority over the community was, in the Old Testament, that of the king, and before him of the Judges; while the Chosen People as a community witnessing to God's truth found its voice in the Prophets. We must see the anointing of the king and the vocation of the prophet as included within the priesthood of the New Law, while the greatest forerunner of all lies outside the general historical structure of the Chosen People altogether. The writer of the Epistle to the Hebrews sees the priesthood of Christ as foreshadowed less by the priesthood of Aaron, whose sacrifices were done away with by Christ's coming, than by that of the priest-king Melchisedech, a figure who appears for a moment in the Book of Genesis (14.18–20), meeting Abraham on his return from victorious battle, "bringing forth bread and wine", blessing Abraham and receiving tribute from him. As a union of priest and king, we find him in the messianic Psalm 109: "The Lord hath sworn and he will not repent: thou art a priest for ever according to the order of Melchisedech". As sharers in the priesthood of Christ, the Church applies these words to all her ordained priests. The three aspects of the New Testament priesthood meet in Melchisedech: he is both priest and king, and as a foreshadowing type of Christ he has the note of prophecy as well.

Christ instituted the New Testament priesthood in his apostles. Ordination, by the laying-on of hands, is simply the reproducing in other men, first by the Apostles and then by their successors, of what Christ made the Apostles in the first place. He made them rulers in charge of the welfare of his church; teachers of his truth to the whole world; and priests appointed to offer his sacrifice.

As those placed in charge of the welfare of the Church, as shepherds of the flock, the

Apostles are judges and stewards (Matt. 19.28: 24.45–51), with authority from heaven to bind and to loose. (Matt. 18.18.) They are given administration of the sacraments for the building up of the Church, being commanded to baptize, to heal the sick, and authorized to forgive and retain sins.

The authority to teach the whole world, as witnesses to God's truth, was given directly to the Apostles. (Matt. 28.16–20; Acts 1.8.) The guarantee that their teaching will remain a witness to the truth lies in the promise that the Spirit will lead them into all truth (John 14.26: 16.13) and the promise of Christ's own presence throughout all time to come (Matt. 28.20); and these promises were made simply to the Apostles. It is by being united, in the communion of one Church, with those who are, by the laying-on of hands, what the Apostles were, that lay Christians share in the task of witnessing to the truth, sacramentally appointed to that task by confirmation.

Finally, at the Last Supper our Lord gave his apostles the power to offer, sacramentally, his own sacrifice. It was as the body and blood of the sacrificial victim that he made his body and blood present in the signs of the bread and wine; they are the body which is given for us, the blood which is shed to seal the new alliance between God and man, as the blood of victims offered at Sinai sealed the first alliance. (Exod. 24.4–8.) Hence when the Apostles fulfilled his command to "do this in commemoration of me", they were making him present as sacrificial victim, making his sacrifice present in the life of the Church and thus sharing intimately in the priesthood of Christ.

As in all the sacraments, it is the consummation of Christ's work in his death and resurrection and the sending forth of the Holy Spirit which fills his appointment and authorization of the Apostles with the vital power that brings their priesthood to life. The Church that they are to rule and nourish comes into existence on Calvary, born into the world by Christ's redemptive act. Their mission to teach the world is only to be begun when that redemptive act is completed in the sending of the Spirit. (Acts 1.8.) And the sacramental sacrifice which they offer is, precisely, the making present of the whole redemptive act, death, resurrection and ascension, in its sacrificial aspect.

Again, as in all the sacraments, while the priesthood is rooted in the historical acts of Christ and operates in the day-to-day life of the Church, it looks forward to the consummation of Christ's second coming. The Judges administer the kingdom in expectation of the Judge who is the King himself, who will make a reckoning with his stewards for good or ill;

the teaching of all nations is to continue "until
the consummation of the world"; and the sacramental sacrifice is a showing forth of the
Lord's death "until he come". (1 Cor. 11.26.)
Like marriage, the sacrament of orders exists
directly for the service of the body of Christ
as a society. Christian marriages build up the
membership of the body by natural generation
and the care and upbringing of children; the
priesthood builds it up by supernatural generation and by fostering and developing the supernatural life. Thus in each of them there is a
living image—in natural parenthood, and in
spiritual fatherhood—of the fatherhood of God
"from whom all fatherhood in heaven and on
earth is named". (Eph. 3.15.) Both social sacraments have a particular concern with the
building-up of the body of Christ which is St.
Paul's theme in the fourth chapter of his letter
to the Ephesians; a continuous growth until
human history is completed by the completion
of the body, grown to its full stature in unity
with its Head: "Until we all meet into the
unity of faith, and of the knowledge of the Son
of God, unto a perfect man, unto the measure
of the age of the fulness of Christ." (Eph. 4.13.)

The sacrament of orders is the laying-on of
hands, begun by the Apostles themselves, by
which a man is made what the Apostles were.

But this summary statement needs much qualification and clarification. First, there was one
essential quality in the Apostles, without which
a man could not be called an Apostle, which
of necessity was not handed on by them.
Namely, they were eyewitnesses of the risen
Christ, as well as being commissioned by him
to bear testimony to him, to teach in his name.
St. Paul realized fully that his own right to
call himself an Apostle as truly as the Twelve
rested on his having seen the risen Lord, too,
on the Damascus road. The successors of the
Apostles by the laying-on of hands are commissioned, as they were, to bear witness to
Christ, teaching in his name; but they cannot,
in the nature of things, be also eyewitnesses of
his risen body. That is an essential quality in
the Apostles themselves which necessarily cannot be part of the apostolic succession. We must
say, then, that ordination makes a man what
the Apostles were except for their character
of eyewitnesses of the risen Lord.

Secondly, the sacrament of orders, as an
initiation into the priesthood of Christ, can
be and is given in different degrees of fullness.
There is a parallel here to the relationship
between the three "sealing" sacraments. Each
of them, baptism, confirmation and orders,
gives a further degree of identification with
Christ the Priest. The third, orders, is itself

conferred in stages; it initiates a man into Christ's priesthood in a greater or lesser degree according to the office in the body of Christ to which he is being appointed. The ordination of a deacon is already the sacrament of orders. It seals a man with a new share in Christ's priesthood, beyond what confirmation gave him. It gives him a new official relationship to the most important of the sacraments; a deacon can baptize, not only privately, in an emergency, as any lay person can, but publicly in the official, liturgical administration of the sacrament; and he can distribute Communion. It gives him, too, a share in the official teaching life of the Church: a deacon could be authorized to preach as part of the liturgy, not only to act as a catechist in the way a lay person can. But this first degree in the sacrament of orders does not give a man the essential priestly power of sacrifice. Only after the second degree of initiation, when the deacon is sacramentally given a further identification with Christ the Priest, do we call him, simply, a priest; one who is able to make Christ's sacrifice sacramentally present. Nor is this, in turn, the fullness of what the sacrament of orders gives. It is the man who is finally consecrated a bishop who is given the fullest possible degree of initiation into Christ's priesthood. We should not think of a bishop as a priest with something added to him beyond the priesthood, but rather as the complete priest, into whose priesthood deacons and priests are partially initiated, to act as the bishop's assistants in ruling, nourishing and teaching the Church. It is of the fullness of orders, as conferred upon the bishop, that we can most truly say that this sacrament is the reproduction in other men, by the laying-on of hands, of what Christ made the Apostles in the first place.

But a third qualification of this description is needed. Each of the Apostles had a relationship to the whole Church which gave his powers a full scope not found in most of their successors. Each of the Apostles was sent by Christ to the whole world (Matt. 28.19); for practical purposes, one might work in one area and another elsewhere, but the mission of each was universal, not restricted. Hence the life of the whole Church, ruling, nourishing, teaching, sacrificing, was in each one. When any Apostle gave formal and definite teaching, he was speaking with the full, infallible authority of the whole Church. But when the apostolic authority was passed on, by the laying-on of hands, it did not, for each man so ordained, include a mission to the whole, universal Church. The ordaining was for a task in one community of the Church, so that the exercise of the apostolic powers which it gave was restricted in scope.

We find St. Paul, for instance, ordaining Timothy and Titus and giving them charge of some area such as Crete (Tit. 1.5) or Ephesus and perhaps neighbouring towns (1 Tim. 1.3.) At the same period, and earlier, groups of presbyters were ordained to be, it seems, jointly in charge of each local Christian community. Fifty years later, in the time of St. Ignatius of Antioch, we find that the pattern has settled down to that of a single bishop, ruling each local church with the powers of an Apostle, and a group of presbyters associated with him performing the subordinate tasks of the ministry. This is roughly the pattern we still have today, only that the community ruled by the bishop is spread over a considerable area through which his presbyters (priests) are scattered, so that they perform, in their parishes, much of the teaching and sacramental work which would in St. Ignatius' time have been performed chiefly, if not exclusively, by the bishop himself.

When a man is ordained priest, he is given a share in the apostolic character by virtue of which men administer God's kingdom, his household, his flock, as judges, stewards and shepherds. But his share in that character remains limited unless the Church goes on to appoint him to a ruling position, the ordinary form of which is nowadays that of bishop of a diocese, and to consecrate him with the fullness of sacramental orders. He then has authority to rule the Church, but only within that diocese. Only one of the Apostles' successors has the universal jurisdiction which each of the Apostles had; the Bishop of Rome, in whom full apostolic authority is continued because he is successor to St. Peter, who held authority even amongst the Apostles themselves.

Again, the seal of ordination numbers a man amongst the teachers in the Church, preaching with apostolic authority. But a priest exercises this authority only under licence from the bishop, and even a bishop does not, individually, teach with the fullness of divinely guaranteed authority which each Apostle had. For each Apostle, having a universal mission, taught with the whole authority of God's church, safeguarded by the Holy Spirit; whereas the bishop's authority to teach is limited to one community in the Church, like his authority to rule. Hence we hear the infallible voice of the whole Church only when the bishops are teaching together as a body, either in the unison of their steady, common teaching or when specially gathered in a General Council; or, again, when the Church speaks through the mouth of the only one of her bishops who has in himself the universal mission each Apostle had—the Pope.

When we come to the power to administer the sacraments, we find a difference in the case of each one. Two of them, in any case, do not require apostolic powers, baptism and marriage. In the case of the others, it seems that the man who is ordained priest, initiated in a degree only less than a bishop into the priesthood of Christ, henceforward has within himself the power to administer all of them except orders itself; but that he can only exercise this power as far as the Church authorizes him to do so.

There are two of the sacraments for which a priest has his powers fully and freely from his ordination day: the Eucharist, and anointing of the sick. If either is performed by a validly ordained priest, even though he may have actually apostatized, it is valid so long as he intends to perform the Christian rite in question. It is as though, in baptism, which can be performed by anybody, and the Eucharist, which can be performed by any priest, there is something in the very nature of the Church which makes it impossible for her to restrict them to the point of ever invalidating them. Somewhat as a human person is free to choose this or that, good or bad, in wise or unwise efforts to be happy, but cannot help wishing to be happy, for it is part of his very nature; so the Church cannot but will to bring forth children, cannot but will to sacrifice, no matter through whom the act is done.[1]

When it comes to the sacrament of penance, the priest's power to absolve, received at ordination, can normally only be validly used when he is authorized to use it by the bishop whose diocese he is in. The power is there, but the man not only may not, but cannot, use it except under licence, called "faculties". Where it is a question of absolving a person in danger of death, any priest available (even if he happens to be excommunicated) automatically has faculties for the occasion, but apart from this, absolution given by a priest is not only unlawful but invalid (that is, it simply is not the sacrament), unless he has faculties for the diocese where he is absolving.

The sacrament of confirmation is under similar but closer restriction. In the West, only bishops ordinarily confirm; but a priest can be specially authorized to do so, and any parish priest can confirm a person in danger of death, so anxious is the Church that a person shall not die without being thus further initiated,

[1] This refers solely to the *validity*, the effective reality, not to the lawfulness of the sacraments. The Church does not *allow* a lay person to baptize except in danger of death when a priest cannot be had. There are many circumstances in which a priest is not *allowed* to say Mass. So if these things are done, in disobedience, they involve sin; but they are still valid, still truly the sacraments and the sacrifice.

beyond baptism, into Christ's priesthood. The power to confirm is given, we see, at ordination, but it not only may not but cannot be exercised except with a further, and in this case exceptional, authorization.

But when we come to the power to ordain, it seems that it is only the man who has, as bishop, been given the fullness of all that the sacrament of orders can give, who can in turn communicate this sacrament to others. There are, it is true, two puzzling cases in the late Middle Ages of Popes specially authorizing abbots of monasteries to ordain their own monks; but they are so sheerly exceptions against the background of the Church's practice all down the ages that it seems more likely that some misunderstanding has arisen over the actual documents, or even that the Pope exceeded his powers and gave permission for something to be done which actually could not be done, than that simple ordination to the priesthood gives a power to ordain which has never been recognized at any other time. It is the final fullness of the priesthood, the complete initiation into Christ's priesthood given in consecration as a bishop, which gives the power to communicate the priesthood to other men. And, once given, it is irrevocable. Even if he separates himself from the communion of the Church, a bishop can still, by virtue of the fullness of the priesthood which he has been given, validly administer all the sacraments. He can still validly ordain priests: he can even validly consecrate other bishops.

In the laying-on of hands which is orders a man is sealed so as to be, essentially, what the Apostles were, for the sake of the continued life of the Church. It is a sacrament which, like baptism, confirmation and marriage, remains present and active through the years that follow. The *res et sacramentum* is the seal itself; the man is, for good or ill, validly a priest for ever. The sheer reality of grace which flows from it is all that he needs in order to be a holy priest, a priest-saint, growing in personal holiness as an image of Christ before the eyes of Christians and unbelievers, and building up the body of Christ by teaching it, by ruling it, by nourishing and healing it with the sacraments, by lifting it up to God in sacrifice, until it shall have grown to its completion and be fulfilled by the second coming of Christ the High Priest.

7. THE EUCHARIST

The moralizing proverb says that we must eat to live, not live to eat. It is easy to find oneself, quite unintentionally, reversing the verbs so that one hears oneself saying the exact opposite. This mere verbal muddle, however feebly, expresses a truth about eating at its highest level, the sacramental feast of Christ's body and blood. For though the Eucharist, like all the sacraments, exists for eternal life—we eat to live—yet all the rest of the life of the Church on earth finds its goal in the Eucharist: we live to eat. This sacrificial banquet is not just one of the Church's activities, nor even simply the most important one. It is, in itself, the Church being fully and completely herself. All her witnessing to the truth, her life as a community, her life of prayer and sacrament, meet in it as their climax and fulfilment. Here is not only teaching, the word about the Word, but the Word himself, the Truth to whom the witness is borne; not only the assembly of Christians, but Christ himself in whom they are united; not only the power of prayer and the sacraments, stemming from Christ, to unite men with God, but the one Mediator himself in whom men are united with God.

Because the Eucharist is both food and sacrifice, there are two currents of preparation for it in the general life of mankind and in the life of the Chosen People in particular. In both—in mankind in general and in Israel—the two themes of food and sacrifice already often came together before their fulfilment in Christ. But the Eucharist is the fulfilment of both, wherever and however they occur; not only of sacrificial feasts but of all feasts, not only of banquet-sacrifices but of all sacrifices.

Food is not only what man lives on, but, to a great extent, what he puts his work into. A great deal of the accumulated knowledge and art of human civilization goes into its production. The bare necessities of the Christian sacrifice—a piece of bread and a cup of wine—represent not only the fruits of the earth, natural products, but the work of man in all the long cultural development needed to achieve a cultivated field, a mill, an oven, a vineyard, a winepress and a cup. What God uses in this sacrament are both gifts of God and works of man; not only natural things but truly human things.

God gives corn to man, man offers bread to God. This pattern, looking forward to the Eucharist, is already established in the Old Law, where bread and flour were among the gifts ritually offered in the Temple. We can see not only a telling answer to hecklers but already a faint hint of the sacrament to come when our Lord defends his apostles, the priests of the New Law, in their picking and eating of corn on the sabbath, by recalling that David, in his day, satisfied his hunger on the sacred loaves which none but priests were allowed to eat. (Mark 2. 23–28.) The offerings of first-

fruits, of flour and of bread, were foreshadowings of the perfect sacrifice to come.

Israel's danger, during much of its life of
preparation, was of slipping from faith in the
corn-giving God into the cult of the corn-god.
A religion which was woven entirely of the
rhythm of nature, whose gods were simply the
gods of the countryside, immersed in the natural processes of germination and generation,
surrounded Israel on all sides. The easy and
obvious thing was to slide into it too, to accept
natural process as the ultimate divinity, to stop
short at the image of God in the cycle of nature
instead of worshipping, through and beyond it,
the God who is the Giver of all these things.
When we are struck simultaneously by the
fury of the Prophets against the gods of the
countryside, and by the apparent similarity of
the myth of the dying-rising-life-giving corn-
god to the Christian redemption for which
these very prophets were preparing, we may
remember how often, it seems, man's rebellions
against God are, essentially, a false anticipation
of something which is to come, rightly, in its
own time. Fullness of knowledge, and "being
like to God", which Adam and Eve ruinously
snatched at, are precisely God's own plan for
human beings, if only we will patiently allow
him to fulfil it. And the corn-god whose worship was, for the Israelites, the ultimate sin,

was only a pale shadow of the incarnate God who was to take bread and make it his own body; and who said of his own death and burial, "Unless the grain of wheat falling into the ground die, itself remaineth alone. But if it die, it bringeth forth much fruit." (John 12.24–5.)

In the meanwhile, Israel must learn and learn again that it is the Lord who is the Giver of food: "And she did not know that I gave her corn and wine, and oil . . . which they have used in the service of Baal", says God through Osee (2.8.) "Thou waterest the hills . . . that thou mayst bring bread out of the earth, and that wine may cheer the heart of man", sings the author of Psalm 103. And at the beginning of the Book of Ruth, a book whose events are woven of the cornfield and the threshing-floor, we find a phrase which seems to sum up all the rich abundance of Old Testament references to the fruits of the earth, and focus them upon the Eucharist that is to come: Naomi set out to return to her own land, for she had heard that the Lord had visited his people and had given them bread.

God is the feeder of his people, It was he who brought them into a land flowing with milk and honey, where there were corn and wine in abundance. But, most important of all, it was he who fed them in the wilderness with bread from heaven. The manna which the people gathered day by day from the ground about their camp was the daily ration for their journey, after their rescue through the sea, towards the Promised Land. So it is one of the chief types in the Old Testament of the Eucharist as food; the traveller's rations of the redeemed people, the Church, journeying through history to the final promised fulfilment. The things said of the manna enhance, in different ways, its meaning as a type. Psalm 77 and the Book of Wisdom speak of it as the bread of angels; as applied to the manna, an image which suggests a fantasy of god-like beings banqueting above the clouds, but in relation to the Eucharist reminding us that we have here in the form of human food him who is the very life of the angels. The author of the Book of Wisdom, writing less than a century before Christ, gives us the poetical image of manna as tasting to each one like his favourite food; however fanciful in its context, a very moderate image of the spiritual richness of sacramental food. In the prose of the Book of Numbers (Chapters 11 and 21) a very different picture is drawn, but one equally familiar to most of us at the times when living on sacraments, by faith and not sense, becomes a wearisome business; for the people grew heartily, disgustedly, rebelliously—and, of course, when one remem-

6+

bers the whole story, entirely unreasonably—
sick of having nothing, day after day, but that
endless flimsy stuff.

Food is not only a matter of rations; when it
takes the form of a banquet, however modest,
it is also one of the unifying things in the social
life of man. "Companion" means one who eats
with you. What can thus express, foster, and
even bring about unity among men has also
been constantly seen as something which could
even achieve union between men and God. A
sacred feast at which the god himself is present,
sharing in it, is a theme often to be found in
man's attempts to re-establish a harmony between himself and the divine source of life.
God's self-revelation in the Old Testament
made it impossible to see him as, in a literal
sense, participating in the feast; there only
remain, in some of the least-assimilated and
most anthropomorphic Old Testament images,
some hints of such an earlier idea, as for example the good smell that the Lord enjoyed
from the sacrifice of Noe. But the theme of the
sacred, communal feast remains, as a feasting
before the Lord. At the ushering in of the life
of the Chosen People, when the Covenant was
made between God and Israel at Sinai, Moses
and Aaron and seventy chosen representatives
went up on the mountain in the sight of God
and ate and drank in his presence. And at the

other end of Old Testament history, the sacred banquet is one of the images expressing the messianic hope. We find it in the writings of the Qumran Community; looking forward to the Messiah meant looking forward to the messianic banquet. In Psalm 21, the psalm Christ quoted on the Cross, when the psalmist looks beyond desolation and suffering to the salvation which God will give after it, he cries, "The poor shall eat and be filled." The mother of the Messiah hailed the dawn of his age with "He hath filled the hungry with good things." All fantasies of warriors feasting in Valhalla or gods feasting on Olympus find their true fulfilment in the feast of the Messiah who ushers in God's reign on earth, at whose table men are united in brotherhood.

A sacred banquet may well be associated, or more or less identical, with a sacrifice. But what is a sacrifice? It is something which can in no sense be understood except in terms of its fulfilment. We can think about food, in terms of nourishment and companionship, and look forward via such considerations to the eucharistic food which transcends and fulfils all other. But we can see sacrifice only by looking backwards from the Cross; for all acts that can be called sacrifice, whether amongst the Hebrews or elsewhere, can only be seen as attempts, necessarily doomed to failure, to do what only Christ could do. That is, to give oneself totally to God, which is the only adequate worship, the only sufficient expression of one's relationship to him. But this no human person could do; for, apart from any other difficulties, none of us possesses himself completely, so that we cannot completely give ourselves either; you can only give what is yours. Christ, the God-Man, alone, being total owner of himself, could and did in his life and the supreme self-giving of his death perform that act which is truly sacrifice, being a true self-sacrifice.

All other sacrifices, whether pagan or Jewish, could be no more than an unfulfilled striving to do what could not be done. First fruits, the best animal of the flock, a beloved son or daughter—with whatever desperate extravagance the victim was chosen, it could not effect a real self-giving. It could be at best a token, to which God could be gracious in so far as it expressed a human need to give, which he himself was eventually to satisfy; and which he could, and did, in the preparatory revelation of the Old Testament, make into a type pointing to what was to come.

All the sacrifices of the Old Testament are types of Christ's sacrifice. Four stand out especially, of which three are brought before our minds by the Church in the Canon of the Mass.

There is the sacrifice of Abel, accepted by God and offered by one who is the archetype of the innocent slain by the envious. Christ himself said that all such killing of the innocent was summed up in his own death: "From the blood of Abel the just, even unto the blood of Zacharias the son of Barachias, whom you killed between the temple and the altar. Amen I say to you, all these things shall come upon this generation." (Matt. 23.35–6.) But while the blood of Abel could only cry out for vengeance, for the kind of justice which remedies evil only by perpetuating it (Gen. 4. 11, 15, 24), the blood of Jesus calls down upon the earth the reign of God's own justice. In him we have come "to the mediator of the new testament, and to the blood which speaketh better than that of Abel". (Heb. 12.24.)

Secondly, there is the sacrifice of Abraham, in which the father of the Chosen People, in unconscious imitation of God the Father, spared not his own son; thirdly, the sacrifice, or at least the priesthood, of Melchisedech; and fourthly, the sacrifice of the paschal lamb.

In the seventh to the tenth chapters of the Epistle to the Hebrews, we are shown how the foreshadowings of the Temple worship are fulfilled and made obsolete by Christ. Animal sacrifices could never cleanse from sin, never make a man truly acceptable to God, and their

inadequacy was even demonstrated by their
endless, daily repetition; when all was done,
all was still to do again. But Christ, being without sin, offering not the blood of goats and
oxen but his own blood, not in any man-made
Temple but in his own body, through the veil
of his own flesh, has offered a truly human
and truly effective sacrifice by which he has
entered not into a symbolic holy place but
into the very presence of God. His priesthood
brings to an end all the mere attempts at
priesthood that foreshadowed it. But the writer
points to one such foreshadowing especially;
Melchisedech, the priest-king to whom Abraham himself did homage, is a prophecy in his
own person of a priesthood superior to that of
Abraham's descendant, Aaron. And when we
turn to Melchisedech in Gen. 14.18–20, we
find that he who foreshadows Christ's priesthood accomplished on the Cross also brings
before our eyes, "bringing forth bread and
wine", the signs under which Christ has left
his one all-sufficient sacrifice sacramentally
amongst us.

The other great type of Christ's sacrifice,
and in many ways the most important, is the
Passover. Just as that greatest of events in the
history of Israel is a type of baptism, so it is
a type of the Eucharist; and both for the one
reason that it is a type of the redemption, of

Christ's own passover from this life to glorified life. Mankind is rescued from the dominion of the devil and set upon its journey towards heaven, as a redeemed and priestly people, just as Israel was rescued from the dominion of Pharaoh and set upon its journey towards the Promised Land as a redeemed and priestly nation. When death and destruction were let loose upon Egypt, the redeemed people were sealed against it by the blood of the lamb which each household had sacrificed, as redeemed humanity is sealed by the blood of Christ, our Pasch, sacrificed for us. The lamb itself was to be eaten as nourishment for the first stage of the journey, so that even before we come to the manna we already have a type of the Eucharist as the wayfarer's food; with the hastily-prepared rations of unleavened bread which the people took with them reminding us of the sign under which it was to be given. But not only was the one great historical event a foreshadowing of Christ; it was to be re-enacted in the ritual Passover year after year in Israel, which prepares us for the sacramental re-enactment of Christ's passover day after day in the Church. And as that sacrament of the Old Law looked forward, however unconsciously, to the coming of Christ as well as back to the Exodus, so the Eucharist in the New Law looks forward to his second coming as well as back to his crucifixion and resurrection.

Each thread woven into the whole has long been prepared when Christ comes to gather them together in himself. He alone can offer the perfect sacrifice; he will preside at a messianic banquet at which he is not only the host but the feast; he will provide food for travellers which is not only given by God but is God himself.

His preparation for this sacrament begins with his very entry into the world. For the first stage in giving us his flesh and blood to be our food and drink was to take flesh and blood from Mary; while the writer of the Epistle to the Hebrews expressly tells us to look at his entry into the world as the beginning of his sacrifice, putting into his mouth one version of the thirty-ninth psalm: "Sacrifice and oblation thou wouldest not: but a body thou hast fitted to me." The bodies of animals were offered in vain, but at last a body can be offered which is the perfect sacrificial victim.

When Christ first came forth in public, John the Baptist pointed to him as the Lamb of God who takes away the sin of the world (John 1.29); the victim of sacrifice, and especially reminiscent of the Passover. One of Christ's own first acts, in all probability, was to purge the Temple of buying and selling, and at the same time to drive out the sacrificial animals from it, perhaps as a sign that their day was over.

(John 2.14–21.) Most significant, here, is his response to the challenge made on this occasion for a sign justifying his action: "Destroy this temple, and in three days I will raise it up . . . But [says St. John] he spoke of the temple of his body." The day of the man-made Temple is over, as Christ tells the Samaritan woman (John 4.21), though it is still so sacred, for the sake of what it has been, that it is worthy of Christ's wrathful cleansing. But the true Temple has come, not made with hands, the body of Christ in which the one perfect sacrifice will be offered for which the Temple sacrifices were only a preparation.

Throughout his ministry, Christ is preparing the Eucharist under its aspect of a feast of friends. He begins his public work at a wedding-feast; constantly delights to be at feasts with every kind of man, so that he is reproached for eating with sinners and for being himself a glutton and a wine-bibber; and tells parables in which the final coming of God which he has come to proclaim is shown in the form of a wedding-feast or a great supper. He sums it up in his words to the Apostles at the Last Supper: "I dispose to you, as my Father hath disposed to me, a kingdom; that you may eat and drink at my table, in my kingdom." (Luke 22.29–30.) Not only that supper itself, but certainly also the meals eaten with the Apostles after the

6*

Resurrection, were realizations of that messianic banquet. They remained in the memory of the Apostles as an essential part of the life of the risen Christ to which they were to bear witness. St. Peter, preaching to Cornelius and his household, refers to the Apostles as those "who did eat and drink with him after he rose again from the dead". (Acts 10.41.) When the very first Christians in Jerusalem came together "in the communication of the breaking of bread" (Acts 2.42), they may well have been remembering those Resurrection meals, in which "they knew him in the breaking of bread", in which he shared fish and honey with them in the upper room or gave them fish by the sea-shore, as much as the Last Supper itself. But we can also see that, in that last feast together before he suffered, everything else, both from before and from after the Resurrection, was brought together and focused; everything is summed up in the meal in which he gave the sacramental sacrifice itself.

Before he came to that fulfilment, he made yet another preparation for it. He explicitly took up and referred to himself the giving of the manna in the old days in the desert. The very fact of his feeding the crowd with bread in the wilderness was already a reminder and fulfilment of the manna as a type. It was also a messianic banquet. Indeed, the people recognized it as such, but, translating it in their minds in terms of their mistaken notion of a political messiah, they took it as a signal to try by force to make him king. (John 6.15.) But Christ did not only point to this fulfilment of the manna by the miraculous act of feeding; he also made it the occasion, next day, for a verbal explanation of how he was going to give an even greater fulfilment to that foreshadowing food. (John 6.26–67.)

He gave this eucharistic teaching in a discourse which passes from teaching about himself as the Life, under the figure of bread, into a direct announcement of the sacrament itself. Both parts raised murmurs among his listeners, but for different reasons. In the first, he was calling on them to go beyond the preoccupation with physical nourishment from which they had started. Even where it was the direct and miraculous gift of God, like manna in the desert, it could only sustain natural life. What we should desire is that life which is eternal, in which we shall be raised up at the last day; and this life is Christ himself. Hence, "I am the bread of life: he that cometh to me shall not hunger: and he that believeth in me shall never thirst." (Verse 35.) Here, indeed, "the bread of life" can be understood as a figure of speech, reminding us of "I am the door of the sheepfold" and "I am the vine". His listeners seem to have understood it as such. They objected, indeed, but not, at this stage, to the idea of his being bread. What they rejected was the claim that he had come down from heaven —he, a man whose family background they knew. Our Lord, in rebuking them, simply makes the same call for faith in himself that he made on many other occasions.

Then he returns to the theme of bread: "Your fathers did eat manna in the desert, and are dead . . . I am the living bread which came down from heaven. If any man eat of this bread, he shall live forever." Is this still a figure of speech? It *could* be. But then, at verse 52, something that can no longer be taken as a figure of speech makes its appearance. Our Lord has been speaking hitherto of the *end*, which is eternal life: and since he himself is that life, we must have him, to live it, as men must have bread to live naturally. But now he begins to speak explicitly of the sacramental *means* to that end; the physical means by which he is going to give himself to his disciples to be their life. "The bread that I will give is my flesh, for the life of the world." The moment that this is said, the objection of his listeners changes to the concrete question, "How can this man give us his flesh to eat?" They have recognized the change from a figurative to a literal meaning.

At first, the only help Christ will give them is, so as to remove all possibility of misunderstanding, to stress and restress the literalness: "Truly I say to you: except you eat the flesh of the Son of man, and drink his blood, you shall not have life in you. He that eateth my flesh and drinketh my blood hath everlasting life: and I will raise him up in the last day. For my flesh is meat indeed and my blood is drink indeed" (the archaism of the Douai translation is not very helpful here; we should do better with "For my flesh really is food and my blood really is drink"). "He that eateth my flesh and drinketh my blood, abideth in me, and I in him. As the living Father hath sent me, and I live by the Father; so he that eateth me, the same also shall live by me. This is the bread that came down from heaven. Not as your fathers did eat manna, and are dead. He that eateth this bread, shall live forever."

For those who complained that this was a hard saying, and who could bear it, he added a word more: "It is the spirit that quickeneth: the flesh profiteth nothing. The words that I have spoken to you are spirit and life." We can see two lessons in this. First, that it is not any cannibalistic feasting on dead flesh of which he was speaking; the body that we eat in the Eucharist is the risen, glorified body, "quickened in the spirit", and risen up again to "where he was before", heaven itself. And second, that we can receive no meaning, no life from Christ's words by any natural power of our own (what the New Testament habitually calls "flesh"), but only by the power of the Spirit granting us the gift of faith. In other words, those who make the first objection ("How can he have come down from heaven?") are bound to make the second ("How can he give us his flesh to eat?"). Whereas those who have a complete faith in Christ as the Son of God can equally accept his gift of himself as food. As St. Peter said at the end of this chapter, when Christ asked the Apostles if they, like the rest, were now going to leave him, "Lord, to whom shall we go? Thou hast the words of eternal life. And we have believed and have known, that thou art the Christ, the Son of God."

When all the lines of preparation were complete; when he had been proclaimed by John the Baptist, and had proclaimed himself, as the victim and temple of the new sacrifice; when he had taught of the messianic feast in parable, and had allowed men a foretaste of it at Cana (where his change of water to wine is even a foretaste of the future change of wine to his blood), and in the houses of his friends, and on the mountain-side; when he had shown that the manna in the wilderness was a prophetical sign of himself, the living bread—then he drew it all together in the Last Supper, and gave us the sacrament in which we have the fulfilment of all these things.

He recalled the different types of his sacrifice again—"With desire I have desired to eat this pasch with you before I suffer" (Luke 22.15)—and told them that his blood was the blood of the new alliance (Matt. 26.28; Mark 14.24; Luke 22.20); as the old alliance at Sinai had been sealed in the blood of sacrificial victims, with which the people were sprinkled, so this new alliance was sealed in the blood of the one true victim, in which his people are washed of their sins.

"And taking bread, he gave thanks, and brake; and gave to them, saying: This is my body, which is given for you. Do this for a commemoration of me. In like manner the chalice also, after he had supped, saying: This is the chalice, the new testament in my blood, which shall be shed for you." (Luke 22.19–20.) St. Matthew's record adds, ". . . which shall be shed for many unto remission of sins." (26.28.)

We have here, then, at the table of the Last Supper, the body and blood of the sacrificial victim: the body "given for you", the blood "shed for many unto remission of sins": and we have them under the signs of bread and wine. Next day, Christ was to undergo bloody and painful death, and in his willing submission to that death he consummated his total self-giving, as man, to God the Father, he himself the priest offering himself the victim in the one true sacrifice. There on Calvary it was enacted as a single historical event; visible and unrepeatable, a part of the time-series of human history. Here in the upper room it was enacted sacramentally; the same priest, offering himself as he did on the Cross, but under the signs of bread and wine instead of through the experience of bodily destruction. Why did he do both? Why perform sacramentally that evening what he was to perform historically next day? Because he could say of the sacramental sacrifice, as he could not of the historical, "Do this for a commemoration of me."

He, our high priest, is "always living to make intercession for us", having "an everlasting priesthood" (Heb. 7.24–5); he is present in heaven as our priest and our victim—a lamb living, and yet as it were slain, as the Apocalypse shows him. (5.6.) His sacrifice is a past historical event, in so far as it happened on Calvary on a Friday in April nineteen hundred and thirty years ago; it is a permanent, everlasting reality in so far as it is presented before the eternal God; but it is needful for us that it should also be a constantly present reality in our day-to-day lives, so that we can join in the offering of it and in being offered in it. This is accomplished, by Christ's own dispensation, by its sacramental representation, in which the one same unrepeatable sacrifice is made really present for us under the signs of bread and wine. By this means, Christ's members on earth, gathered together to offer the sacrifice, can make their offering of praise, prayer and thanksgiving, their offerings of themselves and their whole lives, in union with Christ's offering of himself, made sacramentally present so that it is our act as well as his.

I am going to consider three particular points about the Eucharist here, before attempting to sum up its meaning for us as sacrament and sacrifice.

First, transubstantiation. Christ made the bread his body, the wine his blood; so he said at the Last Supper ("This is my body"), and so he had promised ("The bread which I will give is my flesh"). To say "This is my body", "This is my blood", in Christ's time, and in Christ's language, meant to say, in different ways and with different emphases, "This is my self". Not "part of myself", but simply "myself". It is one aspect when "This is my body" is said: "Myself, broken for you, strengthening you, uniting you in myself"; and another when "This is my blood" is said: "Myself poured out in sacrifice for you, delighting and cheering you as wine cheers the heart of man", for the idea of blood and wine as figures of each other was already an Old Testament idea. But in either case it means "This is myself"; this is, simply, Christ. If we consider, as the Church has considered, the change in the bread and the wine which this implies, we see that nothing can do justice to Christ's words except a *total* change; that the whole of what was bread, the whole of what was wine, is now Christ. Now, this change of the whole into the whole is something that does not occur in the natural order at all. We live, indeed, in a world of change; everything is constantly changing. But there is also, persisting through all changes, always some permanent element. Either something changes, developing or deteriorating, while yet still remaining itself (as a human being, for instance, grows older); or else it is changed so completely that it ceases to be itself, but still some part of it continues, to make a contribution to the thing into which it has been changed. For example, an animal is killed and eaten; it ceases to be itself, but the material components of its body are taken into the bodies of the people who eat it. In the Aristotelian terminology of medieval scholasticism, the *matter* of the pig (for example) persists, but is no longer pig because the *form* of pig has been replaced by the form of human being. The replacement of

one form by another is the most radical and
complete kind of change which can happen by
natural process; the obvious name for it is
transformation. But the change in the Eucharist is no mere transformation; Christ trans-
formed other stuff into the stuff of himself
throughout his life, as all the rest of us do
when we eat, but he was doing nothing of that
sort when he said, "This is my body". Medieval
theologians were not seeing anything new when
they recognized the uniquely total character of
this change. They were seeing it as Christians
had always seen it; as St. Paul saw it when he
said that unworthy eating made the sinner
"guilty of the body and of the blood of the
Lord" (1 Cor. 11.27); as St. Ignatius of Antioch
saw it, fifty years later, when he condemned the
heretics of his day "because they do not admit
that the Eucharist is the flesh of our Saviour
Jesus Christ which suffered for our sins, which
the Father raised up by his goodness" (*Letter
to the Smyrneans*, 6). St. Ambrose, in the fourth
century, was as aware as St. Thomas Aquinas
in the thirteenth that, after consecration, there
is no longer any bread. The contribution of
medieval theology was to supply a word for
this unique change; and the object of inventing
the word was precisely to assert that this change
was like no other. The one truth, the same
since the beginning, which was being asserted

was that here, uniquely, the whole is changed into the whole; and since the current technical term for a "whole" in this sense—a complete individual thing—was "substance", the obvious name for the unique change was tran*substan*-*ti*ation, in contrast to trans*form*ation; for here a whole being has been replaced by a whole being, instead of a form by another form.

St. Thomas Aquinas says, "This is not a formal but a substantial conversion which is not due to any natural movement; it therefore merits a name of its own, and may be called transubstantiation." (*Summa Theologica*, pt. 3, q. 75, art. 3.) The Council of Trent gave its approval when, after reasserting the primitive and unchanging faith of the Church that what happens is the conversion of the whole of the bread into the whole of the body of Christ, the whole of the wine into the whole of his blood, it declared that "transubstantiation" is a suitable name for this conversion.

The whole is converted into the whole; but we continue to see only bread and wine. This miraculous preservation by God's power of the appearances ("accidents" is the scholastic technical term) is a wonder in its own right. For all such qualities in the world around us— bulk, colour, taste, chemical composition, everything that can be reached by measurement and analysis—are by no means a kind of inessential screen floating between us and the real beings (substances) of this world, so that we may know their qualities by sense-experience, but never themselves. On the contrary, these qualities are the essential self-expression of substances; they are the beings themselves in action, and by them we know the beings themselves. But here, in the Eucharist, there is the self-expression of bread, but no bread. God miraculously preserves everything that is implied by the bread, yet the whole of it has become the body of Christ. It is not at all that these qualities are now qualities of Christ. He is not small and white and taking up just so much space on this altar here. The only space which he occupies is that in which his glorified body is in heaven. By his mysterious relationship to the bread and wine appearances, which are miraculously preserved, he can be offered, and eaten, and adored, at all the thousands of places all over the world where transubstantiation takes place. There is no tying-down of Christ, no breaking of him when the host is broken, no "prisoner in the tabernacle". It is not that Christ is on the altar in such a way that he would be visible to us, only that he chooses to disguise himself as bread and wine. He is not present in that ordinary, local sense of the word "present". Speaking, that is, with reference to *place*, he is in heaven; but communicating himself really, physically, sacramentally at every eucharistic altar everywhere through the bread and wine *effects* which he has taken to himself by changing the bread and wine *substance* into his own.

God not only preserves the accidents of bread and wine, but gives them, miraculously, the power to do everything which the substances themselves would have done. "The sacramental species are of course accidents; but they have the act and power of substance." (*Summa Theologica*, pt. 3, q. 77, art. 5, ad 2.) Hence the accidents do all, in the way of chemical reaction etc., that the substance would have done; they behave exactly like a real substance. It is they that change, by transformation, into the stuff of our bodies or, when such events exceptionally take place, into the stuff of micro-organisms, ashes, etc. As soon as such transformation takes place, Christ ceases to be present: his substance is related to the appearances of bread and wine, not to anything into which these appearances change.

Transubstantiation was the first of three points. Secondly, let us remember the unity of Mass and Communion. Christ did not institute a sacrifice of bread and wine which might then, as an extra, be eaten and drunk. He gave the sacrifice, in the very moment of giving it, as food and drink, to be eaten and drunk there and then. It is not a sacrifice which leads to a banquet. It is a sacrifice which *is* a banquet; the meal itself is the sacrifice. It is true that if we are by necessity prevented from presence at the sacrifice, we yet share in it by eating the food which was consecrated at it. And it is true that if, while joining in the Mass, we are prevented from communicating, we can still share in the sacrifice by our desire to communicate, which we would fulfil if only we could. But if we slip from this to a division in our minds of the two things, so that Mass becomes simply an act of public worship to which Communion may be added as an extra, or Communion an act of private devotion for which Mass is merely a necessary means; if we accept it as normal that people joining in the sacrifice at one altar should be sent away to be fed at another; if we begin to think of the presence in the tabernacle, or as elevated at Benediction, as the primary meaning of the Blessed Sacrament, forgetting that its primary meaning is sacrificial food, and all other devotion secondary— if we lose sight of the essential unity to turn aside into any of these things, then we are distorting the meaning of Christ's gift. The Church never has and never can let such distortion affect the essence of the Mass. The priest who celebrates must himself, there and then, eat and drink what he has consecrated; he is not allowed to offer the sacrifice except as a meal. For the rest of us, whatever may have become blurred and confused at different periods, the Church has since the Council of Trent made clear her desire that we should enter fully into the unity of the sacrificial meal; that all who are present at the sacrifice should communicate as part of it.

Thirdly, what is the effect of receiving the Eucharist? The *res et sacramentum* in this sacrament, the thing which is achieved so long as consecration is validly performed, even if all present, and the priest himself, are in such bad dispositions that they get no benefit from it, is the real presence of Christ under the appearances of bread and wine. Since that presence is always a sacrificial presence, we may equally say that while the *signum tantum*, the bare sign that anyone could see, is a meal, the *res et sacramentum*, the reality which is still, in its turn, a sign, is a sacrifice. But what does the eating of that reality do for us? Look at our Lord's words recorded by St. John, already quoted: "He that eateth my flesh and drinketh my blood, abideth in me, and I in him. As the living Father hath sent me, and I live by the Father; so he that eateth me, the same also shall live by me." We eat the human body which is the body of God the Son. By this physical act, the deepest divine condescension to our human, animal nature that there could be, we are united with him in his humanity; we abide in him, sharing in the fullness of grace which is his in his human nature. But not only this; by our union with the Son, we share in *his* relationship with the Father, we are sons in the Son. God gives us, not only an abundance of gifts through his humanity, but, by our union with that humanity, he gives us himself. The Holy Trinity dwells in us, raising us by grace to share the life of the Father, in the Son, by the power of the Spirit, and it is this life of the Trinity within us which takes an ever fuller possession of us, so far as we willingly respond, whenever we eat the human flesh of the Son.

But this is still too individual to be an adequate statement of the *res tantum*, the sheer reality, which is the final goal of the Eucharist. For there is a chorus of agreement in the Church that this final goal is the unity of the Church. The Eucharist is the sacrament of unity, and the name "Communion" expresses this. For "Communion" means union with each other in Christ rather than that purely personal and private union with Christ which it is too often taken to mean. The Church is a Communion; a multitude united in this sacrament. For the indwelling of the Trinity given to us through the humanity of

Christ is not given to us separately and individually, but as members one of another in his body, the Church. Hence that eating which deepens the life of the Trinity in each of us is a building up of the corporate life of the whole body, and the meal and the signs by which it is done show forth this meaning of it. As St. Paul said to the Corinthians, "We, being many, are one bread, one body, all that partake of one bread" (1 Cor. 10.17); in the words of a eucharistic prayer of the second, or possibly even of the first century: "As this broken bread was scattered upon the mountains and was gathered together and became one, so let thy Church be gathered together from the ends of the earth into thy kingdom: for thine is the glory and the power through Jesus Christ for ever and ever." (*Didache*, 9.)

Here, in the holiest of all the sacraments, we have, then, the goal of them all: the body of Christ itself, the unity of the Church. We should get away from thinking of seven sacraments, separate items in a list. There is *one* sacrament, the mystery of Christ the incarnate Word, working in many operations: drawing men into himself in baptism and confirmation; building up his body in space and time in orders and marriage; restoring men to full life in himself when they are separated by sin or hindered by sickness. All these flow from the

Eucharist and meet in the Eucharist, because it is not simply one more such operation of Christ, but is Christ himself, the union of men with God; the reality by which all the others operate and for which all the others are working.

It holds this supreme position because in it is present not only the work and power of Christ's redemption, but Christ himself. The key to all the seven, the source of their grace-giving power, is Christ's passover; his passage from this life through the death of the Cross to the glory of the Resurrection and his entry into heaven. In baptism there is present its power as the rebirth of humanity through death to new life; in confirmation and orders, its power, by re-uniting man with God, to obtain the Spirit who makes us witnesses and priests; in penance, its endless power to win forgiveness for the sins which he bore in his own body upon the tree; in anointing of the sick, its power to heal by taking our infirmities upon himself; in marriage, its power, as the marriage of God with man, to create an image of that union in human marriages. But in the Eucharist we have that passover present precisely as the sacrifice which obtained all these graces; and in order that the sacrifice be present, it is necessary that the priest and victim be present. So here we have Christ present not only by his power, as in all the sacraments, but in his own person, bodily. In him we are incorporated into his passover through death to life. We are fed, on the journey we must make through life to complete that transition, on manna which is himself. By our feeding on his flesh we are given the pledge of the redemption of our bodies. While we are, in sacramental sacrifice, showing forth the death of the Lord until he come, we are, by communion in his sacramental body, building up his body, the Church. The goal of it all is that day when the Church, his body, shall be completed in unity, and he will fulfil the promise which is to be realized in our own bodies: "He that eateth my flesh, and drinketh my blood, hath everlasting life: and I will raise him up in the last day."

APPENDIX 1:

THE SACRAMENTS IN THE NEW TESTAMENT

BAPTISM

Jesus said to him: Amen, amen I say to thee, unless a man be born again, he cannot see the kingdom of God. Nicodemus saith to him: How can a man be born when he is old? Can he enter a second time into his mother's womb and be born again? Jesus answered: Amen, amen I say to thee, unless a man be born again of water and the Holy Ghost, he cannot enter into the kingdom of God. That which is born of the flesh, is flesh: and that which is born of the Spirit, is spirit. Wonder not that I said to thee, you must be born again. The Spirit breatheth where he will: and thou hearest his voice, but thou knowest not whence he cometh and whither he goeth: so is every one that is born of the Spirit.　(John 3.3–8)

The eleven disciples went into Galilee, unto the mountain where Jesus had appointed them. And seeing him, they adored: but some doubted. And Jesus coming spoke to them,

saying: All power is given to me in heaven
and in earth. Going therefore teach ye all
nations: baptizing them in the name of the
Father, and of the Son, and of the Holy Ghost;
teaching them to observe all things whatsoever
I have commanded you: and behold I am with
you all days, even to the consummation of the
world. (Matt. 28.16–20)

And he said to them: Go ye into the whole
world and preach the gospel to every creature.
He that believeth and is baptized shall be
saved: but he that believeth not shall be condemned. (Mark 16.15–16)

Know ye not that all we, who are baptized
in Christ Jesus, are baptized in his death? For
we are buried together with him by baptism
into death: that as Christ is risen from the dead
by the glory of the Father, so we also may walk
in newness of life. For if we have been planted
together in the likeness of his death, we shall
be also in the likeness of his resurrection:
knowing this, that our old man is crucified
with him, that the body of sin may be destroyed, to the end that we may serve sin no
longer. (Rom. 6.3–6)

I would not have you ignorant, brethren,
that our fathers were all under the cloud, and
all passed through the sea. And all in Moses
were baptized, in the cloud, and in the sea;

and did all eat the same spiritual food, and all drank the same spiritual drink (and they drank of the spiritual rock that followed them, and the rock was Christ). But with most of them God was not well pleased: for they were over-thrown in the desert ... Now all these things happened to them in figure: and they are writ-ten for our correction. (1 Cor. 10.1–11)

As the body is one, and hath many members; and all the members of the body, whereas they are many, yet are one body: so also is Christ. For in one Spirit were we all baptized into one body, whether Jews or gentiles, whether bond or free: and in one Spirit we have all been made to drink. (1 Cor. 12.12–13)

As many of you as have been baptized in Christ have put on Christ. There is neither Jew nor Greek: there is neither bond nor free: there is neither male nor female. For you are all one in Christ Jesus. (Gal. 3.27–8)

Christ also loved the church, and delivered himself up for it: that he might sanctify it, cleansing it by the laver of water in the word of life: that he might present it to himself a glorious church, not having spot or wrinkle or any such thing, but that it should be holy and without blemish. (Eph. 5.25–7)

Having, therefore, brethren, a confidence in the entering into the Holies by the blood of

Christ, a new and living way which he hath dedicated for us through the veil, that is to say, his flesh, and a high priest over the house of God: let us draw near with a true heart in fullness of faith, having our hearts sprinkled from an evil conscience, and our bodies washed with clean water. (Heb. 10.19–22)

Christ also died once for our sins, the just for the unjust: that he might offer us to God, being put to death indeed in the flesh, but enlivened in the spirit, in which also coming he preached to those spirits that were in prison: which had been some time incredulous, when they waited for the patience of God in the days of Noe, when the ark was a-building: wherein a few, that is, eight souls, were saved by water. Whereunto baptism being of the like form, now saveth you also: not the putting away of the filth of the flesh, but the examination of a good conscience towards God by the resurrection of Jesus Christ. (1 Peter 3.18–21)

CONFIRMATION

Now when the apostles, who were in Jerusalem, had heard that Samaria had received the word of God, they sent unto them Peter and John. Who when they were come prayed for them that they might receive the Holy Ghost. For he was not as yet come upon any of them: but they were only baptized in the name of

the Lord Jesus. Then they laid their hands
upon them: and they received the Holy Ghost.
(Acts 8.14–17)

Paul . . . came to Ephesus and found certain
disciples; and he said to them: Have you received the Holy Ghost since ye believed? But
they said to him: We have not so much as heard
whether there be a Holy Ghost. And he said:
In what then were you baptized? Who said: In
John's baptism. Then Paul said: John baptized
the people with the baptism of penance, saying: That they should believe in him who was
to come after him, that is to say, in Jesus. Having heard these things, they were baptized in
the name of the Lord Jesus. And when Paul
had imposed his hands on them, the Holy Ghost
came upon them: and they spoke with tongues
and prophesied. (Acts 19.1–6)

THE EUCHARIST

Amen, amen, I say unto you: He that believeth in me hath everlasting life. I am the
bread of life. Your fathers did eat manna in
the desert, and are dead. This is the bread
which cometh down from heaven: that if any
man eat of it, he may not die. I am the living
bread which came down from heaven. If any
man eat of this bread, he shall live for ever; and
the bread that I will give, is my flesh for the
life of the world. The Jews therefore strove

7+

among themselves, saying: How can this man give us his flesh to eat? Then Jesus said to them: Amen, amen, I say unto you: Except you eat the flesh of the Son of Man, and drink his blood, you shall not have life in you. He that eateth my flesh and drinketh my blood hath everlasting life: and I will raise him up in the last day. For my flesh is meat indeed: and my blood is drink indeed. He that eateth my flesh and drinketh my blood, abideth in me, and I in him. As the living Father hath sent me, and I live by the Father: so he that eateth me, the same also shall live by me. This is the bread that came down from heaven. Not as your fathers did eat manna, and are dead. He that eateth this bread shall live for ever. These things he said teaching in the synagogue in Capharnaum. Many therefore of his disciples hearing it, said: This saying is hard, and who can bear it? But Jesus knowing in himself that his disciples murmured at this, said to them: Doth this scandalize you? If then you shall see the Son of Man ascend up where he was before? It is the spirit that quickeneth: the flesh profiteth nothing. The words that I have spoken to you are spirit and life. But there are some of you that believe not. For Jesus knew from the beginning who they were that did not believe, and who he was that would betray him. And he said: Therefore did I say to you, that no man can come to me unless it be given him by my Father. After this many of his disciples went back and walked no more with him.

(John 6.47–67)

And whilst they were at supper, Jesus took bread, and blessed, and broke, and gave to his disciples, and said: Take ye, and eat. This is my body. And taking the chalice he gave thanks, and gave to them, saying: Drink ye all of this. For this is my blood of the new testament which shall be shed for many unto remission of sins. And I say to you, I will not drink from henceforth of this fruit of the vine, until that day when I shall drink it with you new in the kingdom of my Father.

(Matt. 26.26–9)

I have received of the Lord that which also I delivered unto you, that the Lord Jesus, the same night in which he was betrayed, took bread, and giving thanks, broke, and said: Take ye and eat: this is my body which shall be delivered for you: this do for the commemoration of me. In like manner also the chalice, after he had supped, saying: This chalice is the new testament in my blood: this do ye, as often as you shall drink, for the commemoration of me. For as often as you shall eat this bread, and drink the chalice, you shall shew the death of the Lord, until he come. Therefore whosoever shall eat this bread, or drink the chalice of the Lord unworthily, shall be guilty of the body and of the blood of the Lord. But let a man prove himself: and so let him eat of that bread, and drink of the chalice. For he that eateth and drinketh unworthily, eateth and drinketh judgment to himself, not discerning the body of the Lord. (1 Cor. 11.23–9)

Wherefore, my dearly beloved, fly from the service of idols. I speak as to wise men: judge ye yourselves what I say. The chalice of benediction which we bless, is it not the communion of the blood of Christ? And the bread which we break, is it not the partaking of the body of the Lord? For we, being many, are one bread, one body, all that partake of one bread. Behold Israel according to the flesh: are not they that eat of the sacrifices partakers of the altar? What then? Do I say that what is offered in sacrifice to idols is any thing? Or that the idol is any thing? But the things which the heathens sacrifice, they sacrifice to devils and not to God. And I would not that you should be made partakers with devils. You cannot drink the chalice of the Lord, and the chalice of devils:

you cannot be partakers of the table of the Lord, and of the table of devils.

(1 Cor. 10.14–21)

PENANCE

If thy brother shall offend against thee, go and rebuke him between thee and him alone. If he shall hear thee, thou shalt gain thy brother. And if he will not hear thee, take with thee one or two more: that in the mouth of two or three witnesses every word may stand. And if he will not hear them: tell the church. And if he will not hear the church, let him be to thee as the heathen and publican. Amen I say to you, whatsoever thou shall bind upon earth shall be bound also in heaven: and whatsoever you shall loose upon earth shall be loosed also in heaven.   (Matt. 18.15–18)

Now when it was late that same day, the first of the week, and the doors were shut, where the disciples were gathered together for fear of the Jews, Jesus came and stood in the midst, and said to them: Peace be to you. And when he had said this he shewed them his hands and his side. The disciples therefore were glad when they saw the Lord. He said therefore to them again: Peace be to you. As the Father hath sent me, I also send you. When he had said this he breathed on them; and he said to them:

Receive ye the Holy Ghost: whose sins you shall forgive, they are forgiven them: and whose sins you shall retain, they are retained.

(John 20.19–23)

It is absolutely heard that there is fornication among you, and such fornication as the like is not among the heathens; that one should have his father's wife . . . I indeed, absent in body, but present in spirit, have already judged, as though I were present, him that hath so done, in the name of our Lord Jesus Christ, you being gathered together, and my spirit, with the power of our Lord Jesus: to deliver such a one to Satan for the destruction of the flesh, that the spirit may be saved in the day of our Lord Jesus Christ.   (1 Cor. 5.1–5)

And if any one have caused grief, he hath not grieved me; but in part, that I may not burden you all. To him that is such a one this rebuke is sufficient, that is given by many: so that contrariwise you should rather pardon and comfort him, lest perhaps such a one be swallowed up with overmuch sorrow. For which cause I beseech you, that you would confirm your charity towards him. For to this end also did I write, that I may know the experiment of you, whether you be obedient in all things. And to whom you have pardoned any thing,

I also. For what I have pardoned, if I have pardoned any thing, for your sakes have I done it in the person of Christ: that we be not over-reached by Satan.   (2 Cor. 2.5–11)
(It is not suggested that these two passages can be assumed to refer to the same man; this, though possible, seems unlikely, as the second one seems rather to imply an injury done personally to St. Paul.)

ANOINTING OF THE SICK

Is any man sick among you? Let him bring in the priests of the church, and let them pray over him, anointing him with oil in the name of the Lord. And the prayer of faith shall save the sick man. And the Lord shall raise him up. And if he be in sins, they shall be forgiven him.
(Jas. 5.14–15)

ORDERS

[*In New Testament usage, the various titles such as "ancient", "priest", "bishop", were not yet being used with a single, precise meaning: "priest" (derived from "presbyter", meaning "elder" or "ancient") might be used for "bishop" and vice versa. It is clear that there were already the different degrees of authority in those ordained, but the habit of using one*

*word always for one degree was not yet estab-
lished.*]

In the church which was at Antioch ... as
they were ministering to the Lord, and fasting,
the Holy Ghost said to them: Separate me Saul
and Barnabas, for the work whereunto I have
taken them. Then they, fasting and praying,
and imposing their hands upon them, sent
them away. 　　　　　　　　(Acts 13.1–3)

And when they had preached the gospel to
that city [Derbe], and had taught many, they
returned again to Lystra and to Iconium and
to Antioch: confirming the souls of the disciples, and exhorting them to continue in the
faith; and that through many tribulations we
must enter into the kingdom of God. And when
they had ordained to them priests in every
church, and had prayed with fasting, they com-
mended them to the Lord, in whom they believed. 　　　　　　　　(Acts 14.20–22)

[Paul], sending from Miletus to Ephesus ...
called the ancients of the church. And when
they were come to him, and were together, he
said to them ... Take heed to yourselves and
to the whole flock, wherein the Holy Ghost
hath placed you bishops, to rule the church of
God which he hath purchased with his own
blood. 　　　　　　　　(Acts 20.17–18, 28)

Obey your prelates and be subject to them:

for they watch as being to render an account of your souls; that they may do this with joy, and not with grief.   (Heb. 13.17)

If a man desire the office of a bishop, he desireth a good work. It behoveth therefore a bishop to be blameless, the husband of one wife . . . one that ruleth well his own house, having his children in subjection with all chastity. But if a man know not how to rule his own house, how shall he take care of the church of God?   (1 Tim. 3.1–5)

These things command and teach. Let no man despise thy youth: but be thou an example of the faithful, in word, in conversation, in charity, in faith, in chastity. Till I come, attend unto reading, to exhortation, and to doctrine. Neglect not the grace that is in thee: which was given thee by prophecy, with imposition of the hands of the priesthood.
                    (1 Tim. 4.11–14)

I admonish thee, that thou stir up the grace of God which is in thee by the imposition of my hands.   (2 Tim. 1.6)

For this cause I left thee in Crete, that thou shouldest set in order the things that are wanting, and shouldest ordain priests in every city, as I also appointed thee: if any be without crime, the husband of one wife, having faithful children, not accused of riot or unruly. For a bishop must be without crime, as the steward of God: not proud, not subject to anger, not given to wine, no striker, not greedy of filthy lucre: but given to hospitality, gentle, sober, just, holy, continent; embracing that faithful word which is according to doctrine, that he may be able to exhort in sound doctrine and to convince the gainsayers.   (Titus 1.5–9)

The ancients therefore that are among you, I beseech, who am myself also an ancient and a witness of the sufferings of Christ, as also a partaker of that glory which is to be revealed in time to come: feed the flock of God which is among you, taking care of it not by constraint, but willingly according to God: not for filthy lucre's sake, but voluntarily: neither as lording it over the clergy, but being made a pattern of the flock from the heart. And when the prince of pastors shall appear, you shall receive a never-fading crown of glory.   (1 Pet. 5.1–4)

MARRIAGE

And there came to him the Pharisees tempting him, saying: Is it lawful for a man to put away his wife for every cause? Who answering, said to them: Have ye not read that he who made man from the beginning, made them male and female? And he said: *For this cause shall a man leave father and mother, and shall cleave to his wife, and they two shall be in one flesh*. Therefore now they are not two, but one flesh. What therefore God hath joined together, let no man put asunder. They say to him: Why then did Moses command to give a bill of divorce and to put away? He saith to them: Because Moses by reason of the hardness of your heart permitted you to put away your wives: but from the beginning it was not so. And I say to you, that whosoever shall put away his wife, except it be for fornication, and shall marry another, committeth adultery; and he that shall marry her that is put away, committeth adultery.   (Matt. 19.3–9)

But I say to the unmarried, and to the widows: it is good for them if they so continue, even as I. But if they do not contain themselves, let them marry. For it is better to marry than to be burnt. But to them that are married, not I, but the Lord, commandeth that the wife depart not from her husband. And if she depart, that she remain unmarried, or be reconciled to her husband. And let not the husband put away his wife.   (1 Cor. 7.8–11)

Let women be subject to their husbands as to the Lord: because the husband is the head of the wife: as Christ is the head of the church. He is the saviour of his body. Therefore as the church is subject to Christ, so also let the wives be to their husbands in all things. Husbands, love your wives, as Christ also loved the church, and delivered himself up for it: that he might sanctify it, cleansing it by the laver of water in the word of life: that he might present it to himself a glorious church, not having spot or wrinkle or any such thing, but that it should be holy and without blemish. So also ought men to love their wives as their own bodies. He that loveth his wife loveth himself. For no man ever hated his own flesh: but nourisheth and cherisheth it, as also Christ doth the church: because we are members of his body, of his flesh, and of his bones. *For this cause shall a man leave his father and mother: and shall cleave to his wife, and they shall be two in one flesh.* This is a great sacrament: but I speak in Christ and in the church. Nevertheless let every one of you in particular love his wife as himself: and let the wife fear her husband.

(Eph. 5.22–33)

APPENDIX 2:

THE SACRAMENTS IN CHRISTIAN WRITINGS OF THE FIRST TWO HUNDRED YEARS

The writers quoted here all belong to the first two centuries of the Church's life, which began in A.D. 30. The earliest of them, Clement, wrote before the death of St. John the Apostle. The latest of them, Origen, was born of Christian parents about 185; those parents could well have been personally acquainted with the personal disciples of an Apostle or Evangelist. For Catholics, the tradition of the Church is an equally living thing in any century, for it lives by the Holy Spirit and not by human memory; nevertheless, it is useful to look at the writings of a time when tradition in the purely human sense of the word was still in such close living and personal touch with its apostolic origins.

The quotations are taken from:

The *Didache*, or "Teaching of the Twelve Apostles", a description of Christian practice which cannot be dated with accuracy but belongs either to the first or the second century;

Clement, Bishop of Rome, third in succession from St. Peter, who wrote a letter to the Corinthians in about A.D. 94;

Ignatius, Bishop of Antioch, who wrote a series of letters to various churches while being taken, a prisoner, to Rome in about 110;

Hermas, who wrote *The Shepherd*, an account of several visions giving an allegorical picture of the Church, written at Rome, probably about 140, though earlier dates have been suggested;

Justin, a gentile convert of Palestine, who taught and wrote at Rome about the middle of the century and was martyred there in 165;

Irenaeus, born about 130 in Asia Minor, Bishop of Lyons from 177 to about 200, author of *Against the Heretics* and *The Apostolic Teaching*, written some time after he became bishop;

Tertullian of Carthage, converted in 193 and the author of many books on Christian belief and practice. His conviction that sexual sin was unforgivable and his admiration for the Montanist "New Prophets" (heretics who claimed private revelations overriding the Church's teaching) took him out of the Church in 213. His very disapproval often makes him a valuable witness to current Catholic belief and practice, e.g., of infant baptism and of absolution for sexual sin;

Origen, born about 185 of Christian parents at Alexandria, died 254 at Caesarea, Palestine, after producing a huge body of theological writings.

THE SACRAMENTAL PRINCIPLE
TERTULLIAN

It is wholly impossible for the soul to be saved if it has not believed while still in the flesh; salvation, indeed, hinges on the flesh. If the soul is received into fellowship with God, it is actually the flesh which makes this possible. The flesh is washed so that the soul may be cleansed; the flesh is anointed so that the soul may be sanctified; the flesh is marked with the sign so that the soul may be strengthened; the flesh is overshadowed with the laying-on of hands so that the soul may be enlightened by the Spirit; the flesh feeds on the body and blood of Christ so that the soul may be nourished with God. United in service, they cannot be divided in reward.

(*On the Resurrection of the Body*, 8)

BAPTISM
THE DIDACHE

Baptize in this way: first repeat all this teaching [i.e., about the Christian way of life], then baptize in the name of the Father and of the Son and of the Holy Ghost, in running water. If you have no running water, baptize in other water; if you cannot baptize in cold water, use warm. If you have neither, pour water on the head three times in the name of the Father and of the Son and of the Holy Ghost. Before baptism, he who is to baptize and the one to be baptized should fast, and any others who can do so; and you are to tell the baptized person to fast for a few days.

IGNATIUS

Our God, Jesus Christ . . . was born, and was baptized in order to purify water through his passion.   (*To the Ephesians*, 18.2)

JUSTIN

All those who accept and believe the things we teach, and who promise that they can live in accordance with them, are taught to pray and beseech God, fasting, to pardon their former sins, while we join with them in prayer and fasting. Then we bring them somewhere where there is water, where they are reborn in the same way that we were: they are washed in the water in the name of God the Father and Lord of all, and of Jesus Christ our Saviour, and of the Holy Ghost. (*Apologia I*, 61)

IRENAEUS

Dry flour cannot be united as a lump of dough, or a loaf, without liquid; so we who are many cannot be made one in Christ Jesus without water from heaven ... For our bodies have, by washing, been given the unity which brings us to immortality; our souls receive it by means of the Spirit. Thus both are needed, for together they further man's advance towards the life of God. (*Against the Heretics*, 3,17,2)

Christ came to save all men through himself: that is to say, all who through him are reborn to God—infants, children, youths, young men and old.   (*Against the Heretics*, 2.22,4)

TERTULLIAN

Just because it is all so simple ... when a man is plunged into water, and dipped, with a few words to accompany it, and then rises up very little cleaner, if at all—just because of this, it seems unbelievable to men that eternal life should be won in such a way ... We wonder at it too, but we wonder at it because we believe it.   (*On Baptism*, 2)

It is better to delay baptism according to the individual's state and character, especially in the case of infants. Why should sponsors, too, have to undergo this danger, when they may fail to carry out their promises because of death, or be disappointed by the child's growing up with a bad character? Yes, the Lord says, "Forbid them not to come to me"; then let them come when they are growing up ... Why does the age of innocence seek forgiveness of sins?

(On Baptism, 18)

ORIGEN

The Church has received from the Apostles the tradition of baptizing infants. For entrusted as they were with the hidden mysteries of God, they knew that in all mankind there are inborn stains of sin which must be washed away by water and the Spirit.

(Commentary on the Epistle to the Romans, 5,9)

Washing in water symbolizes the cleansing of the soul by washing away all the filth that comes from sin; it is also itself the origin and source of divine gifts.

(Commentary on St. John, 6,33)

CONFIRMATION

TERTULLIAN

The angel of baptism "makes straight the paths" for the Holy Spirit who is to come, by washing away sins in response to faith sealed in the Father, the Son and the Holy Spirit.

Afterwards the hand is laid upon us in an act

of blessing through which the Holy Spirit is invoked and invited.   (*On Baptism*, 6 and 8)

THE EUCHARIST
THE DIDACHE

On the Lord's Day come together to break bread and give thanks, first publicly confessing your faults so that your sacrifice may be pure. If anyone has quarrelled with a friend, he may not join the assembly till they are reconciled, lest your sacrifice be defiled. For this is the sacrifice spoken of by the Lord: "In every place and time offer me clean sacrifice." (Mal. 1,11)

IGNATIUS

What I desire is the bread of God, which is the flesh of Jesus Christ of the race of David, and for drink I desire his blood, which is incorruptible love.   (*To the Romans*, 7,3)

Be careful to share in only one Eucharist; for there is only one flesh of our Lord Jesus Christ, and only one cup to unite us with his blood, only one altar, as there is only one bishop with his presbyters and deacons, my fellow-servants.

(*To the Philadelphians*, 4)

They [the heretics] stay away from the Eucharist and from prayer, because they do not believe that the Eucharist is the flesh of our

Saviour Jesus Christ which suffered for our sins and which the Father has, in his goodness, raised up. (*To the Smyrnians*, 7,1)

JUSTIN

We call this food Eucharist, and only those may eat who believe the truth of our teaching, have been washed for the remission of sins and rebirth, and live according to the rule of Christ. We do not take these gifts as ordinary food and drink, but as Jesus Christ our Saviour was made flesh by the word of God, taking flesh and blood for our salvation, so the bread which has been made Eucharist by the word of prayer which came from him, the food which, by its transformation, nourishes our blood and flesh, is, by our teaching, the flesh and blood of the incarnate Jesus. (*Apologia I*, 65–66)

IRENAEUS

The Church alone offers a clean oblation to the Creator, offering to him, with thanksgiving, from his own creation . . . Those [heretics] who say that this created world was made of "corruption, ignorance and passion" sin against their Father by offering him fruits of "ignorance, passion and corruption", an insulting rather than a thankful gesture. How can they consistently think that the bread of the Eucha-

rist is the body of their Lord, and the cup the
cup of his blood, if they say that he is not the
Son of the Creator of the world? ... Again, how
can they say that flesh corrupts and has no share
in life, when flesh is nourished on the body
and blood of the Lord? They should either
change their minds or stop offering these obla-
tions. But our view accords with the Eucharist
and the Eucharist supports our view. We offer
him his own, fitly showing forth the common
unity of flesh and spirit. The bread, coming
from the earth, receives the invocation of God
and is then no longer common bread but
Eucharist, consisting of two things, earthly and
heavenly; so our bodies, after sharing in the
Eucharist, are no longer corruptible but have
the hope of eternal resurrection.

(*Against the Heretics*, 4,18,4–5)

Whenever the cup, mixed by man, and the
bread, made by man, receive the word of God,
the Eucharist becomes the body of Christ, and
by these elements our fleshly substance is
nourished and sustained. Then how can they
[the heretics] maintain that the flesh cannot
receive the gift of God, eternal life, when the
flesh feeds upon the flesh and the blood of the
Lord and is a member of him?

(*Against the Heretics*, 5,2,3)

TERTULLIAN

Many people think that they ought not to take part in the prayers of sacrifice on fast days, because the fast must be broken by taking the Lord's body . . . Will not your fast be all the more solemn if you have stood at God's altar? When the body of the Lord has been received and reserved, then you have both shared in the sacrifice and performed your duty.

(*On Prayer*, 19)

Your husband (if he is a pagan) will not know what you are secretly eating before you take food. Even if he knows it is bread, will he not think it is what it is rumoured to be [by enemies of the Christians who accused them of cannibalism]? (*To His Wife*, 2,5)

ORIGEN

You know with what care and reverence, when you take part in the divine mysteries, you guard the body of the Lord when you receive it, lest the smallest crumb fall to the ground . . . When, as is only right, you are so careful in guarding his body, do you think it less blameworthy to neglect the word of God than his body?

(**Sermon on the Book of Exodus**, 13,3)

PENANCE

HERMAS

"I am the Shepherd to whom thou wast delivered". While he was still speaking, his form was changed and I recognized him as the same to whom I was delivered.

[*Hermas' allegory is often obscure, but the Shepherd seems here to identify himself with Hermas' own bishop. He later continues:*]

The Lord, the discerner of hearts, foreknowing all things, saw the weakness of men and the manifold wiles of the devil, who will always be doing some mischief to the servants of God and dealing wickedly with them. The Lord, then, being very compassionate, had pity on the work of his hands, and appointed this repentance, and to me was given authority over this repentance. But if after this great and holy calling [of baptism] anyone shall, tempted by the devil, commit sin, he has only one repentance. (*The Shepherd*, revelation 5 and mandate 4,3)

IRENAEUS

By such words and deeds [i.e., seduction disguised as spiritual direction] they [the Gnostic heretics] have, in this very district of the Rhone, led astray many women, who have their consciences seared as with a hot iron. Some, indeed, publicly confess their sins; but others are ashamed to do this, despair of the life of God, and, keeping silent, have apostatized altogether: others again hesitate halfway, remaining, as the proverb says, "neither out nor in".

(*Against the Heretics*, 1,13,7)

TERTULLIAN

Since this second and last penance is so serious a matter, it must be tested in a correspondingly exacting way. Hence it must not be performed solely in one's conscience but must also be shown forth in some external act. This act is known by the Greek name of *exomologesis*, by which we confess our sin to the Lord, not that he is ignorant of it but because satisfaction is begun by confession, confession produces penitence and by penitence God is appeased . . . This discipline bids the sinner go about in sackcloth and ashes . . . to nourish prayers with fasting, to mourn and weep and groan day and night to the Lord his God, to prostrate himself before the priest, to kneel to the beloved of God, to ask all the brethren to sponsor his prayer for mercy . . . By humbling the sinner it raises him up; by making him filthy it cleanses him; by accusing and condemning him it absolves him. Be sure that God will spare you just so far as you do not spare yourself.   (*On Penance*, 9)

Since you know that *exomologesis* is a second defence against hell, supporting the first line of defence, the Lord's baptism, why do you abandon the means of salvation? . . . Will the sinner knowingly despise *exomologesis*, which has been instituted by God for his restoration?
(*On Penance*, 12)

That supreme pontiff, bishop of bishops [the Bishop of Rome], proclaims: "I absolve those who have done penance for adultery and fornication"! . . . Where will they publish this generosity? Outside brothels, I imagine, under the signs of their trade . . . But this edict is read in the churches, proclaimed in the Church, the Church who is a virgin!   (*On Purity*, 1)

But, you say, the Church has power to remit sins? I have every reason to agree and assert the same thing, since I find the Paraclete saying through the New Prophets: "The Church has power to remit sin; but I will not, lest they commit further sins."   (*On Purity*, 21)

ORIGEN

There is only one opportunity of repentance granted for more serious offences; but the ordinary faults which we frequently incur can always be repented and are continually being redeemed.

(*Sermon on the Book of Leviticus,* 15)

If we have sinned we ought also to say, "I have acknowledged my sin to thee, and my injustice I have not concealed. I said I will confess against myself my injustice to the Lord." [Ps. 31.5.] For if we do this and declare our sins not only to God but also to those who can heal us of our wounds and sins, our wickedness will be wiped out by him who says "I will blot out thy iniquities as a cloud." [Is. 44.22.]

(*Sermon on St. Luke,* 17)

Perhaps members of the Church who listen to this [about the different sin-offerings] may say, "Those men of Old Testament times were better off . . . For us there is only one pardon for sins, given at the start by the grace of the font; afterwards there is no mercy for sinners, no forgiveness". A Christian certainly ought to be under stricter discipline, since Christ died for him . . . Yet, lest these considerations should lead you to despair rather than rouse you to virtue, listen to all the ways of remission of sins in the Gospels. First we are baptized . . . [(2) martyrdom; (3) works of mercy; (4) by forgiveness of others; (5) by conversion of a sinner; (6) by abundance of love] . . . There is a seventh way of forgiveness, though hard and painful, which is the remission of sins by penance, when the sinner "washes his bed with his tears" [Ps. 6.7] and "his tears are his bread day and night" [Ps. 41,4], and when he does not shrink in shame from declaring his sin to the priest of the Lord and asking for medicine.

(*Homily on the Book of Leviticus*, 2,4)

The layman cannot get rid of his sins on his own . . . He must have a priest or even someone of higher rank; he needs the High Priest, the Pontiff, if he is to have his sin remitted . . . It is the saints who do penance for their sins. They it is who feel their wounds, seek out a priest and ask for healing and cleansing from the Pontiff.

(*Homily on the Book of Numbers*, 10,1)

ORDERS

CLEMENT

The Lord has ordered that offerings and services should be done with care, at fixed times and seasons, not at random and irregularly . . . The high priest has his own special tasks, the priests have been allotted their place, the Levites are appointed to their special services. The layman is bound by the rules that apply to the laity.   (*To the Corinthians*, 40)

Through our Lord Jesus Christ our Apostles knew, moreover, that there would be disagreement about the bishop's office. So, having complete foreknowledge, they appointed these persons [the bishops] and then provided, further, that if they should fall asleep other tried men should succeed them in their office. When, therefore, men appointed by the Apostles, or later by other notable men, with the approval of the whole community, have blamelessly served the flock of Christ, with humble heart, peacefully and honourably, with good reports from all sides for long periods, we think it unjust to depose them from their office. For it will be no light sin on our part if we depose from the bishop's office those who have blamelessly and in a holy manner offered the gifts.   (*To the Corinthians*, 44)

IGNATIUS

All of you follow the bishop, as Jesus Christ follows his Father, and the presbyters as the Apostles; as for the deacons, respect them as the law of God. Let no one do anything regarding the Church apart from the bishop. Let only that Eucharist be regarded as lawful which is done under the presidency of the bishop or of one whom he has appointed. Where the bishop appears, there let the community be, just as where Jesus Christ is, there is the Catholic Church. Apart from the bishop, it is not per-

mitted to baptize nor hold an agape, but all
that he approves is also pleasing to God. Thus
all that is done will be safe and lawful.

(*To the Smyrnians*, 8,1–2)

IRENAEUS

We have a duty to obey the presbyters who
are in the Church, having their succession from
the Apostles, who with that episcopal succession have received with certainty the spiritual
gift of truth according to the Father's good
pleasure. As for others, who, wherever they
may assemble together, stand apart from that
primitive succession, we should regard them
with suspicion. (*Against the Heretics*, 1,26,2)

TERTULLIAN

The chief priest, that is to say, the bishop,
has the right to baptize; after him, the presbyters and deacons, but only by the authority
of the bishop . . . The laity too have the right,
for what has been received equally by all can
be given equally by all . . . But . . . "All things
are permitted, but not all things are expedient", says the blessed Apostle. Be content, then,
to use your right in cases of necessity, when the
special nature of place, time or person demands
it.   (*On Baptism*, 17)

A woman may neither preach, baptize, make

the offering nor claim any masculine office, least of all that of a priest.

(On the Veiling of Virgins, 9)

ORIGEN

"Moses gathered together the congregation and said: This is the word that the Lord hath commanded." Though the Lord had commanded the appointment of the high priest and had chosen him, yet the congregation is summoned too. For at the ordination of a priest the presence of the people is required so that all may be certain that the man chosen for the priesthood is of all the people the most eminent, learned, holy and outstanding in every virtue. This must be done with the people present so as to avoid later changes or hesitations of mind.

(Sermon on the Book of Leviticus, 6,3)

MARRIAGE

IGNATIUS

When men and women are marrying it is well that they should make their contract with the consent of the bishop, so that their marriage may be according to the Lord and not according to passion. *(To Polycarp,* 5,2)

TERTULLIAN

How can we ever sufficiently describe the happiness of that marriage which is brought about by the Church, strengthened by the sacrifice, sealed by the blessing, at which angels act as witnesses and to which the Father gives his consent?   (*To His Wife*, 8)